Project Control Stages
Complete Self-Assessment Guide

The guidance in this Self-Assessment is b;
best practices and standards in business ;
and quality management. The guidance i;
judgment of the individual collaborators listed in the Acknowledgments.

Notice of rights

Trademarks

Table of Contents

About The Art of Service

The Art of Service, Business Process Architects since 2000, is dedicated to helping stakeholders achieve excellence.

Defining, designing, creating, and implementing a process to solve a stakeholders challenge or meet an objective is the most valuable role… In EVERY group, company, organization and department.

Unless you're talking a one-time, single-use project, there should be a process. Whether that process is managed and implemented by humans, AI, or a combination of the two, it needs to be designed by someone with a complex enough perspective to ask the right questions.

Someone capable of asking the right questions and step back and say, 'What are we really trying to accomplish here? And is there a different way to look at it?'

With The Art of Service's Standard Requirements Self-Assessments, we empower people who can do just that — whether their title is marketer, entrepreneur, manager, salesperson, consultant, Business Process Manager, executive assistant, IT Manager, CIO etc... —they are the people who rule the future. They are people who watch the process as it happens, and ask the right questions to make the process work better.

Contact us when you need any support with this Self-Assessment and any help with templates, blue-prints and examples of standard documents you might need:

http://theartofservice.com
service@theartofservice.com

Acknowledgments

This checklist was developed under the auspices of The Art of Service, chaired by Gerardus Blokdyk.

Representatives from several client companies participated in the preparation of this Self-Assessment.

In addition, we are thankful for the design and printing services provided.

Included Resources - how to access

Included with your purchase of the book is the Project Control Stages Self-Assessment Spreadsheet Dashboard which contains all questions and Self-Assessment areas and auto-generates insights, graphs, and project RACI planning - all with examples to get you started right away.

How? Simply send an email to
access@theartofservice.com
with this books' title in the subject to get the Project Control Stages Self Assessment Tool right away.

You will receive the following contents with New and Updated specific criteria:

- The latest quick edition of the book in PDF

- The latest complete edition of the book in PDF, which criteria correspond to the criteria in...

- The Self-Assessment Excel Dashboard, and...

- Example pre-filled Self-Assessment Excel Dashboard to get familiar with results generation

- In-depth specific Checklists covering the topic

- Project management checklists and templates to assist with implementation

INCLUDES LIFETIME SELF ASSESSMENT UPDATES

Every self assessment comes with Lifetime Updates and Lifetime Free Updated Books. Lifetime Updates is an industry-first feature which allows you to receive verified self assessment updates, ensuring you always have the most accurate information at your fingertips.

Get it now- you will be glad you did - do it now, before you forget.

Send an email to **access@theartofservice.com** with this books' title in the subject to get the Project Control Stages Self Assessment Tool right away.

Project Control Stages Scorecard

Your Scores:

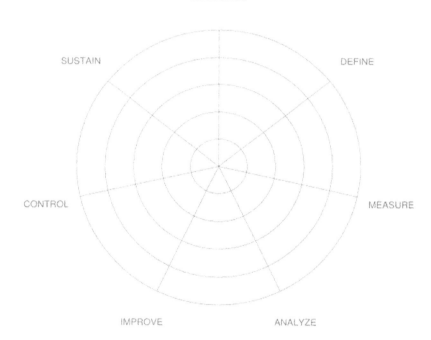

BEGINNING OF THE SELF-ASSESSMENT:

CRITERION #1: RECOGNIZE

INTENT: Be aware of the need for change. Recognize that there is an unfavorable variation, problem or symptom.

In my belief, the answer to this question is clearly defined:

5 Strongly Agree

4 Agree

3 Neutral

2 Disagree

1 Strongly Disagree

1. Does our organization need more Project Control Stages education?
<--- Score

2. How do you assess your Project Control Stages workforce capability and capacity needs, including skills, competencies, and staffing levels?
<--- Score

3. How much are sponsors, customers, partners, stakeholders involved in Project Control Stages? In other words, what are the risks, if Project Control Stages does not deliver successfully?
<--- Score

4. What is the smallest subset of the problem we can usefully solve?
<--- Score

5. Who else hopes to benefit from it?
<--- Score

6. Is it clear when you think of the day ahead of you what activities and tasks you need to complete?
<--- Score

7. What should be considered when identifying available resources, constraints, and deadlines?
<--- Score

8. What problems are you facing and how do you consider Project Control Stages will circumvent those obstacles?
<--- Score

9. How can we tell when PC is needed?
<--- Score

10. What vendors make products that address the Project Control Stages needs?
<--- Score

11. Will a response program recognize when a crisis occurs and provide some level of response?

<--- Score

47. How does it fit into our organizational needs and tasks?
<--- Score

48. Why do we need to keep records?
<--- Score

49. How do you identify the kinds of information that you will need?
<--- Score

50. What are the expected benefits of Project Control Stages to the stakeholder?
<--- Score

51. Are there recognized Project Control Stages problems?
<--- Score

Add up total points for this section:
_ _ _ _ _ = Total points for this section

Divided by: _ _ _ _ _ _ (number of statements answered) = _ _ _ _ _ _ Average score for this section

Transfer your score to the Project Control Stages Index at the beginning of the Self-Assessment.

CRITERION #2: DEFINE:

INTENT: Formulate the stakeholder problem. Define the problem, needs and objectives.

In my belief, the answer to this question is clearly defined:

5 Strongly Agree

4 Agree

3 Neutral

2 Disagree

1 Strongly Disagree

1. What organizational structure is required?
<--- Score

2. Has a team charter been developed and communicated?
<--- Score

3. What customer feedback methods were used to solicit their input?

<--- Score

4. Are task requirements clearly defined?
<--- Score

5. What are the compelling stakeholder reasons for embarking on Project Control Stages?
<--- Score

6. Is the Project Control Stages scope manageable?
<--- Score

7. Are accountability and ownership for Project Control Stages clearly defined?
<--- Score

8. Has the Project Control Stages work been fairly and/or equitably divided and delegated among team members who are qualified and capable to perform the work? Has everyone contributed?
<--- Score

9. Does the team have regular meetings?
<--- Score

10. What are the rough order estimates on cost savings/opportunities that Project Control Stages brings?
<--- Score

11. Is a fully trained team formed, supported, and committed to work on the Project Control Stages improvements?
<--- Score

12. Have the customer needs been translated into

specific, measurable requirements? How?
<--- Score

13. Is there a completed SIPOC representation, describing the Suppliers, Inputs, Process, Outputs, and Customers?
<--- Score

14. Have all basic functions of Project Control Stages been defined?
<--- Score

15. Who are the Project Control Stages improvement team members, including Management Leads and Coaches?
<--- Score

16. Are different versions of process maps needed to account for the different types of inputs?
<--- Score

17. Are approval levels defined for contracts and supplements to contracts?
<--- Score

18. How do you keep key subject matter experts in the loop?
<--- Score

19. When are meeting minutes sent out? Who is on the distribution list?
<--- Score

20. How often are the team meetings?
<--- Score

21. Is full participation by members in regularly held team meetings guaranteed?
<--- Score

22. What is the minimum educational requirement for potential new hires?
<--- Score

23. Is there a completed, verified, and validated high-level 'as is' (not 'should be' or 'could be') stakeholder process map?
<--- Score

24. Has the improvement team collected the 'voice of the customer' (obtained feedback – qualitative and quantitative)?
<--- Score

25. Is the CR within project scope?
<--- Score

26. Is there a Project Control Stages management charter, including stakeholder case, problem and goal statements, scope, milestones, roles and responsibilities, communication plan?
<--- Score

27. How is the team tracking and documenting its work?
<--- Score

28. How will variation in the actual durations of each activity be dealt with to ensure that the expected Project Control Stages results are met?
<--- Score

29. Is there regularly 100% attendance at the team meetings? If not, have appointed substitutes attended to preserve cross-functionality and full representation?
<--- Score

30. What constraints exist that might impact the team?
<--- Score

31. Is the team formed and are team leaders (Coaches and Management Leads) assigned?
<--- Score

32. Is the team equipped with available and reliable resources?
<--- Score

33. When was the Project Control Stages start date?
<--- Score

34. How and when will the baselines be defined?
<--- Score

35. What tools and roadmaps did you use for getting through the Define phase?
<--- Score

36. Are customers identified and high impact areas defined?
<--- Score

37. Is there a critical path to deliver Project Control Stages results?
<--- Score

38. How would you define the culture here?
<--- Score

39. Have all of the relationships been defined properly?
<--- Score

40. Has the direction changed at all during the course of Project Control Stages? If so, when did it change and why?
<--- Score

41. Are there different segments of customers?
<--- Score

42. Is Project Control Stages currently on schedule according to the plan?
<--- Score

43. Has anyone else (internal or external to the group) attempted to solve this problem or a similar one before? If so, what knowledge can be leveraged from these previous efforts?
<--- Score

44. Will team members regularly document their Project Control Stages work?
<--- Score

45. Will team members perform Project Control Stages work when assigned and in a timely fashion?
<--- Score

46. Is the improvement team aware of the different versions of a process: what they think it is vs. what it actually is vs. what it should be vs. what it could be?

<--- Score

47. What defines Best in Class?
<--- Score

48. Has a project plan, Gantt chart, or similar been developed/completed?
<--- Score

49. What would the requirements look like?
<--- Score

50. Why is it required?
<--- Score

51. What specifically is the problem? Where does it occur? When does it occur? What is its extent?
<--- Score

52. When is the estimated completion date?
<--- Score

53. Is the scope of Project Control Stages defined?
<--- Score

54. What are the Roles and Responsibilities for each team member and its leadership? Where is this documented?
<--- Score

55. How can the value of Project Control Stages be defined?
<--- Score

56. How did the Project Control Stages manager receive input to the development of a Project

Control Stages improvement plan and the estimated completion dates/times of each activity?
<--- Score

57. What key stakeholder process output measure(s) does Project Control Stages leverage and how?
<--- Score

58. Are there any constraints known that bear on the ability to perform Project Control Stages work? How is the team addressing them?
<--- Score

59. What are the boundaries of the scope? What is in bounds and what is not? What is the start point? What is the stop point?
<--- Score

60. Are team charters developed?
<--- Score

61. How will the Project Control Stages team and the group measure complete success of Project Control Stages?
<--- Score

62. Is the current 'as is' process being followed? If not, what are the discrepancies?
<--- Score

63. Have specific policy objectives been defined?
<--- Score

64. Are customer(s) identified and segmented according to their different needs and requirements?
<--- Score

65. Is data collected and displayed to better understand customer(s) critical needs and requirements.
<--- Score

66. Has a high-level 'as is' process map been completed, verified and validated?
<--- Score

67. If substitutes have been appointed, have they been briefed on the Project Control Stages goals and received regular communications as to the progress to date?
<--- Score

68. Are audit criteria, scope, frequency and methods defined?
<--- Score

69. Is the team adequately staffed with the desired cross-functionality? If not, what additional resources are available to the team?
<--- Score

70. Is Project Control Stages Required?
<--- Score

71. In what way can we redefine the criteria of choice clients have in our category in our favor?
<--- Score

72. Is Project Control Stages linked to key stakeholder goals and objectives?
<--- Score

73. How do senior leaders promote an environment that fosters and requires legal and ethical behavior?
<--- Score

74. In what way can we redefine the criteria of choice in our category in our favor, as Method introduced style and design to cleaning and Virgin America returned glamor to flying?
<--- Score

75. Are security/privacy roles and responsibilities formally defined?
<--- Score

76. Has/have the customer(s) been identified?
<--- Score

77. How does the Project Control Stages manager ensure against scope creep?
<--- Score

78. Are stakeholder processes mapped?
<--- Score

79. What are the dynamics of the communication plan?
<--- Score

80. Are improvement team members fully trained on Project Control Stages?
<--- Score

81. How would one define Project Control Stages leadership?
<--- Score

82. Are Required Metrics Defined?
<--- Score

83. Do we all define Project Control Stages in the same way?
<--- Score

84. Are roles and responsibilities formally defined?
<--- Score

85. What would be the goal or target for a Project Control Stages's improvement team?
<--- Score

86. What baselines are required to be defined and managed?
<--- Score

87. Who defines (or who defined) the rules and roles?
<--- Score

88. Has everyone on the team, including the team leaders, been properly trained?
<--- Score

89. Is the team sponsored by a champion or stakeholder leader?
<--- Score

90. Is it clearly defined in and to your organization what you do?
<--- Score

91. How was the 'as is' process map developed, reviewed, verified and validated?

<--- Score

92. What critical content must be communicated –
who, what, when, where, and how?
<--- Score

93. Do the problem and goal statements meet the
SMART criteria (specific, measurable, attainable,
relevant, and time-bound)?
<--- Score

Add up total points for this section:
_____ = Total points for this section

Divided by: _____ (number of
statements answered) = _____
Average score for this section

Transfer your score to the Project
Control Stages Index at the beginning of
the Self-Assessment.

CRITERION #3: MEASURE:

INTENT: Gather the correct data.
Measure the current performance and
evolution of the situation.

In my belief, the answer to this
question is clearly defined:

5 Strongly Agree

4 Agree

3 Neutral

2 Disagree

1 Strongly Disagree

1. What are the agreed upon definitions of the high
impact areas, defect(s), unit(s), and opportunities that
will figure into the process capability metrics?
<--- Score

2. How is progress measured?
<--- Score

3. What Relevant Entities could be measured?

<--- Score

4. Why Measure?
<--- Score

5. What are my customers expectations and measures?
<--- Score

6. How large is the gap between current performance and the customer-specified (goal) performance?
<--- Score

7. Are we taking our company in the direction of better and revenue or cheaper and cost?
<--- Score

8. Do staff have the necessary skills to collect, analyze, and report data?
<--- Score

9. What potential environmental factors impact the Project Control Stages effort?
<--- Score

10. What are our key indicators that you will measure, analyze and track?
<--- Score

11. Is there a Performance Baseline?
<--- Score

12. How frequently do we track measures?
<--- Score

13. How frequently do you track Project Control

Stages measures?
<--- Score

14. What is measured?
<--- Score

15. What measurements are possible, practicable and meaningful?
<--- Score

16. Have all non-recommended alternatives been analyzed in sufficient detail?
<--- Score

17. How can you measure Project Control Stages in a systematic way?
<--- Score

18. Are process variation components displayed/ communicated using suitable charts, graphs, plots?
<--- Score

19. What methods are feasible and acceptable to estimate the impact of reforms?
<--- Score

20. Customer Measures: How Do Customers See Us?
<--- Score

21. Are key measures identified and agreed upon?
<--- Score

22. Why should we expend time and effort to implement measurement?
<--- Score

23. How do you identify and analyze stakeholders and their interests?

<--- Score

24. Is this an issue for analysis or intuition?

<--- Score

25. How will effects be measured?

<--- Score

26. Is it possible to estimate the impact of unanticipated complexity such as wrong or failed assumptions, feedback, etc. on proposed reforms?

<--- Score

27. Is Process Variation Displayed/Communicated?

<--- Score

28. How to measure lifecycle phases?

<--- Score

29. How do we do risk analysis of rare, cascading, catastrophic events?

<--- Score

30. How are you going to measure success?

<--- Score

31. Are high impact defects defined and identified in the stakeholder process?

<--- Score

32. What are your key Project Control Stages organizational performance measures, including key short and longer-term financial measures?

<--- Score

33. How do you measure success?
<--- Score

34. Have the concerns of stakeholders to help identify and define potential barriers been obtained and analyzed?
<--- Score

35. Which Stakeholder Characteristics Are Analyzed?
<--- Score

36. What is the total cost related to deploying Project Control Stages, including any consulting or professional services?
<--- Score

37. Is long term and short term variability accounted for?
<--- Score

38. What are the costs of reform?
<--- Score

39. How will you measure your Project Control Stages effectiveness?
<--- Score

40. How to measure variability?
<--- Score

41. What should be measured?
<--- Score

42. What key measures identified indicate the performance of the stakeholder process?

<--- Score

43. Are the measurements objective?
<--- Score

44. How Will We Measure Success?
<--- Score

45. Do we effectively measure and reward individual and team performance?
<--- Score

46. How is the value delivered by Project Control Stages being measured?
<--- Score

47. Was a data collection plan established?
<--- Score

48. Does Project Control Stages analysis isolate the fundamental causes of problems?
<--- Score

49. Does the practice systematically track and analyze outcomes related for accountability and quality improvement?
<--- Score

50. What measurements are being captured?
<--- Score

51. How do we focus on what is right -not who is right?
<--- Score

52. What is the right balance of time and resources

between investigation, analysis, and discussion and dissemination?
<--- Score

53. Meeting the challenge: are missed Project Control Stages opportunities costing us money?
<--- Score

54. What will be measured?
<--- Score

55. What evidence is there and what is measured?
<--- Score

56. Can we do Project Control Stages without complex (expensive) analysis?
<--- Score

57. Are you taking your company in the direction of better and revenue or cheaper and cost?
<--- Score

58. What data was collected (past, present, future/ongoing)?
<--- Score

59. What are the types and number of measures to use?
<--- Score

60. When is Knowledge Management Measured?
<--- Score

61. Which customers can't participate in our market because they lack skills, wealth, or convenient access to existing solutions?

<--- Score

62. What charts has the team used to display the components of variation in the process?
<--- Score

63. Which customers cant participate in our Project Control Stages domain because they lack skills, wealth, or convenient access to existing solutions?
<--- Score

64. Are there any easy-to-implement alternatives to Project Control Stages? Sometimes other solutions are available that do not require the cost implications of a full-blown project?
<--- Score

65. What is measured?
<--- Score

66. What about Project Control Stages Analysis of results?
<--- Score

67. Do we aggressively reward and promote the people who have the biggest impact on creating excellent Project Control Stages services/ products?
<--- Score

68. Does Project Control Stages analysis show the relationships among important Project Control Stages factors?
<--- Score

69. Why do measure/indicators matter?

<--- Score

70. How will success or failure be measured?
<--- Score

71. What are measures?
<--- Score

72. Among the Project Control Stages product and service cost to be estimated, which is considered hardest to estimate?
<--- Score

73. What are the key input variables? What are the key process variables? What are the key output variables?
<--- Score

74. What are the uncertainties surrounding estimates of impact?
<--- Score

75. Which methods and measures do you use to determine workforce engagement and workforce satisfaction?
<--- Score

76. How are measurements made?
<--- Score

77. Where is it measured?
<--- Score

78. Does the Project Control Stages task fit the client's priorities?
<--- Score

79. Is a solid data collection plan established that includes measurement systems analysis?
<--- Score

80. Are losses documented, analyzed, and remedial processes developed to prevent future losses?
<--- Score

81. Have you found any 'ground fruit' or 'low-hanging fruit' for immediate remedies to the gap in performance?
<--- Score

82. How will your organization measure success?
<--- Score

83. What particular quality tools did the team find helpful in establishing measurements?
<--- Score

84. What to measure and why?
<--- Score

85. Are there measurements based on task performance?
<--- Score

86. Is the solution cost-effective?
<--- Score

87. What has the team done to assure the stability and accuracy of the measurement process?
<--- Score

88. Are the units of measure consistent?
<--- Score

89. Have the types of risks that may impact Project Control Stages been identified and analyzed?
<--- Score

90. Is data collection planned and executed?
<--- Score

91. Is key measure data collection planned and executed, process variation displayed and communicated and performance baselined?
<--- Score

92. How will measures be used to manage and adapt?
<--- Score

93. Who participated in the data collection for measurements?
<--- Score

94. Will We Aggregate Measures across Priorities?
<--- Score

95. Why do the measurements/indicators matter?
<--- Score

96. Why identify and analyze stakeholders and their interests?
<--- Score

97. Does Project Control Stages systematically track and analyze outcomes for accountability and quality improvement?
<--- Score

98. What is an unallowable cost?

<--- Score

99. Can We Measure the Return on Analysis?
<--- Score

100. Have changes been properly/adequately analyzed for effect?
<--- Score

101. Is performance measured?
<--- Score

102. How do senior leaders create a focus on action to accomplish the organization s objectives and improve performance?
<--- Score

103. Who should receive measurement reports ?
<--- Score

104. How can we measure the performance?
<--- Score

105. How is Knowledge Management Measured?
<--- Score

106. Is data collected on key measures that were identified?
<--- Score

107. Are priorities and opportunities deployed to your suppliers, partners, and collaborators to ensure organizational alignment?
<--- Score

Add up total points for this section:

_____ = Total points for this section

Divided by: _____ (number of
statements answered) = _____
Average score for this section

Transfer your score to the Project
Control Stages Index at the beginning of
the Self-Assessment.

CRITERION #4: ANALYZE:

INTENT: Analyze causes, assumptions and hypotheses.

In my belief, the answer to this question is clearly defined:

5 Strongly Agree

4 Agree

3 Neutral

2 Disagree

1 Strongly Disagree

1. Identify an operational issue in your organization. for example, could a particular task be done more quickly or more efficiently?
<--- Score

2. How was the detailed process map generated, verified, and validated?
<--- Score

3. What tools were used to generate the list of

49

possible causes?
<--- Score

4. What conclusions were drawn from the team's data collection and analysis? How did the team reach these conclusions?
<--- Score

5. Record-keeping requirements flow from the records needed as inputs, outputs, controls and for transformation of a Project Control Stages process. ask yourself: are the records needed as inputs to the Project Control Stages process available?
<--- Score

6. Were any designed experiments used to generate additional insight into the data analysis?
<--- Score

7. What successful thing are we doing today that may be blinding us to new growth opportunities?
<--- Score

8. Do our leaders quickly bounce back from setbacks?
<--- Score

9. Think about the functions involved in your Project Control Stages project. what processes flow from these functions?
<--- Score

10. Did any additional data need to be collected?
<--- Score

11. Are gaps between current performance and the

goal performance identified?
<--- Score

12. What quality tools were used to get through the analyze phase?
<--- Score

13. What are your current levels and trends in key measures or indicators of Project Control Stages product and process performance that are important to and directly serve your customers? how do these results compare with the performance of your competitors and other organizations with similar offerings?
<--- Score

14. What tools were used to narrow the list of possible causes?
<--- Score

15. Where is the data coming from to measure compliance?
<--- Score

16. What are the revised rough estimates of the financial savings/opportunity for Project Control Stages improvements?
<--- Score

17. Was a cause-and-effect diagram used to explore the different types of causes (or sources of variation)?
<--- Score

18. Is the Project Control Stages process severely broken such that a re-design is necessary?
<--- Score

19. What are the best opportunities for value improvement?
<--- Score

20. What did the team gain from developing a sub-process map?
<--- Score

21. What process should we select for improvement?
<--- Score

22. How is the way you as the leader think and process information affecting your organizational culture?
<--- Score

23. Do you, as a leader, bounce back quickly from setbacks?
<--- Score

24. What are the disruptive Project Control Stages technologies that enable our organization to radically change our business processes?
<--- Score

25. What were the crucial 'moments of truth' on the process map?
<--- Score

26. When conducting a business process reengineering study, what should we look for when trying to identify business processes to change?
<--- Score

27. What are your current levels and trends in key

Project Control Stages measures or indicators of product and process performance that are important to and directly serve your customers?
<--- Score

28. What is the cost of poor quality as supported by the team's analysis?
<--- Score

29. Is the suppliers process defined and controlled?
<--- Score

30. How often will data be collected for measures?
<--- Score

31. How do mission and objectives affect the Project Control Stages processes of our organization?
<--- Score

32. Was a detailed process map created to amplify critical steps of the 'as is' stakeholder process?
<--- Score

33. Have the problem and goal statements been updated to reflect the additional knowledge gained from the analyze phase?
<--- Score

34. How do you use Project Control Stages data and information to support organizational decision making and innovation?
<--- Score

35. What are our Project Control Stages Processes?
<--- Score

36. Think about some of the processes you undertake within your organization. which do you own?
<--- Score

37. Have any additional benefits been identified that will result from closing all or most of the gaps?
<--- Score

38. How does the organization define, manage, and improve its Project Control Stages processes?
<--- Score

39. A compounding model resolution with available relevant data can often provide insight towards a solution methodology; which Project Control Stages models, tools and techniques are necessary?
<--- Score

40. Is the gap/opportunity displayed and communicated in financial terms?
<--- Score

41. What does the data say about the performance of the stakeholder process?
<--- Score

42. What were the financial benefits resulting from any 'ground fruit or low-hanging fruit' (quick fixes)?
<--- Score

43. Were there any improvement opportunities identified from the process analysis?
<--- Score

44. Can we add value to the current Project Control Stages decision-making process (largely qualitative) by incorporating uncertainty modeling (more quantitative)?
<--- Score

45. Is the performance gap determined?
<--- Score

46. Is Data and process analysis, root cause analysis and quantifying the gap/opportunity in place?
<--- Score

47. How do we promote understanding that opportunity for improvement is not criticism of the status quo, or the people who created the status quo?
<--- Score

48. An organizationally feasible system request is one that considers the mission, goals and objectives of the organization. key questions are: is the solution request practical and will it solve a problem or take advantage of an opportunity to achieve company goals?
<--- Score

49. Is the suppliers process defined and controlled?
<--- Score

50. Do your employees have the opportunity to do what they do best everyday?
<--- Score

51. How do you measure the Operational performance of your key work systems and processes, including productivity, cycle time, and other appropriate measures of process effectiveness, efficiency, and innovation?
<--- Score

52. Did any value-added analysis or 'lean thinking' take place to identify some of the gaps shown on the 'as is' process map?
<--- Score

53. What other organizational variables, such as reward systems or communication systems, affect the performance of this Project Control Stages process?
<--- Score

54. Were Pareto charts (or similar) used to portray the 'heavy hitters' (or key sources of variation)?
<--- Score

55. What controls do we have in place to protect data?
<--- Score

56. What other jobs or tasks affect the performance of the steps in the Project Control Stages process?
<--- Score

Add up total points for this section:
_ _ _ _ _ = Total points for this section

Divided by: _ _ _ _ _ _ (number of statements answered) = _ _ _ _ _ _
Average score for this section

Transfer your score to the Project
Control Stages Index at the beginning of
the Self-Assessment.

CRITERION #5: IMPROVE:

INTENT: Develop a practical solution.
Innovate, establish and test the
solution and to measure the results.

In my belief, the answer to this
question is clearly defined:

5 Strongly Agree

4 Agree

3 Neutral

2 Disagree

1 Strongly Disagree

1. Are new and improved process ('should be') maps
developed?
<--- Score

**2. What should a proof of concept or pilot
accomplish?**
<--- Score

3. Describe the design of the pilot and what tests were

conducted, if any?
<--- Score

4. How does the solution remove the key sources of issues discovered in the analyze phase?
<--- Score

5. Are improved process ('should be') maps modified based on pilot data and analysis?
<--- Score

6. Who will be responsible for making the decisions to include or exclude requested changes once Project Control Stages is underway?
<--- Score

7. How do you improve workforce health, safety, and security? What are your performance measures and improvement goals for each of these workforce needs and what are any significant differences in these factors and performance measures or targets for different workplace environments?
<--- Score

8. Are there any constraints (technical, political, cultural, or otherwise) that would inhibit certain solutions?
<--- Score

9. Risk factors: what are the characteristics of Project Control Stages that make it risky?
<--- Score

10. At what point will vulnerability assessments be performed once Project Control Stages is put into

production (e.g., ongoing Risk Management after implementation)?
<--- Score

11. Do we cover the five essential competencies-Communication, Collaboration,Innovation, Adaptability, and Leadership that improve an organization's ability to leverage the new Project Control Stages in a volatile global economy?
<--- Score

12. How can we improve Project Control Stages?
<--- Score

13. How do we measure improved Project Control Stages service perception, and satisfaction?
<--- Score

14. Is there a cost/benefit analysis of optimal solution(s)?
<--- Score

15. What attendant changes will need to be made to ensure that the solution is successful?
<--- Score

16. How do we Improve Project Control Stages service perception, and satisfaction?
<--- Score

17. Are we Assessing Project Control Stages and Risk?
<--- Score

18. What lessons, if any, from a pilot were incorporated into the design of the full-scale solution?
<--- Score

19. If you could go back in time five years, what decision would you make differently? What is your best guess as to what decision you're making today you might regret five years from now?
<--- Score

20. Is pilot data collected and analyzed?
<--- Score

21. How do you measure progress and evaluate training effectiveness?
<--- Score

22. Risk events: what are the things that could go wrong?
<--- Score

23. What is Project Control Stages's impact on utilizing the best solution(s)?
<--- Score

24. What is the implementation plan?
<--- Score

25. What communications are necessary to support the implementation of the solution?
<--- Score

26. How do we go about Comparing Project Control Stages approaches/solutions?
<--- Score

27. Were any criteria developed to assist the team in testing and evaluating potential solutions?
<--- Score

28. Is a contingency plan established?
<--- Score

29. What does the 'should be' process map/design look like?
<--- Score

30. What are the implications of this decision 10 minutes, 10 months, and 10 years from now?
<--- Score

31. How can skill-level changes improve Project Control Stages?
<--- Score

32. Does the goal represent a desired result that can be measured?
<--- Score

33. Why improve in the first place?
<--- Score

34. How do we improve productivity?
<--- Score

35. How will the group know that the solution worked?
<--- Score

36. How significant is the improvement in the eyes of the end user?
<--- Score

37. What were the underlying assumptions on the cost-benefit analysis?

<--- Score

38. Can the solution be designed and implemented within an acceptable time period?
<--- Score

39. How to Improve?
<--- Score

40. Is a solution implementation plan established, including schedule/work breakdown structure, resources, risk management plan, cost/budget, and control plan?
<--- Score

41. What actually has to improve and by how much?
<--- Score

42. Are the best solutions selected?
<--- Score

43. What tools were most useful during the improve phase?
<--- Score

44. Who controls key decisions that will be made?
<--- Score

45. How do we decide how much to remunerate an employee?
<--- Score

46. What is risk identification?
<--- Score

47. How does the team improve its work?

<--- Score

48. In the past few months, what is the smallest change we have made that has had the biggest positive result? What was it about that small change that produced the large return?
<--- Score

49. Is the implementation plan designed?
<--- Score

50. What tools were used to tap into the creativity and encourage 'outside the box' thinking?
<--- Score

51. What is a risk review?
<--- Score

52. Who controls the risk?
<--- Score

53. What to do with the results or outcomes of measurements?
<--- Score

54. What tools were used to evaluate the potential solutions?
<--- Score

55. How will you know when its improved?
<--- Score

56. How can we improve performance?
<--- Score

57. How do we measure risk?

<--- Score

58. Who are the people involved in developing and implementing Project Control Stages?
<--- Score

59. What can we do to improve?
<--- Score

60. How will the team or the process owner(s) monitor the implementation plan to see that it is working as intended?
<--- Score

61. Who will be responsible for documenting the Project Control Stages requirements in detail?
<--- Score

62. What is the team's contingency plan for potential problems occurring in implementation?
<--- Score

63. Do we get business results?
<--- Score

64. What evaluation strategy is needed and what needs to be done to assure its implementation and use?
<--- Score

65. What is the magnitude of the improvements?
<--- Score

66. Was a pilot designed for the proposed solution(s)?
<--- Score

67. What do we want to improve?
<--- Score

68. How will you know that you have improved?
<--- Score

69. How Do We Link Measurement and Risk?
<--- Score

70. Is the measure understandable to a variety of people?
<--- Score

71. What improvements have been achieved?
<--- Score

72. What actually has to improve and by how much?
<--- Score

73. What error proofing will be done to address some of the discrepancies observed in the 'as is' process?
<--- Score

74. What resources are required for the improvement effort?
<--- Score

75. What needs improvement?
<--- Score

76. How do we keep improving Project Control Stages?
<--- Score

77. Are possible solutions generated and tested?

<--- Score

78. How do you improve your likelihood of success ?
<--- Score

79. How did the team generate the list of possible solutions?
<--- Score

80. How do the Project Control Stages results compare with the performance of your competitors and other organizations with similar offerings?
<--- Score

81. For decision problems, how do you develop a decision statement?
<--- Score

82. Is the solution technically practical?
<--- Score

83. What is the risk?
<--- Score

84. How do you use other indicators, such as workforce retention, absenteeism, grievances, safety, and productivity, to assess and improve workforce engagement?
<--- Score

85. How will we know that a change is improvement?
<--- Score

86. What went well, what should change, what can improve?

<--- Score

87. For estimation problems, how do you develop an estimation statement?
<--- Score

88. Is the optimal solution selected based on testing and analysis?
<--- Score

89. Is there a high likelihood that any recommendations will achieve their intended results?
<--- Score

90. To what extent does management recognize Project Control Stages as a tool to increase the results?
<--- Score

91. How important is the completion of a recognized college or graduate-level degree program in the hiring decision?
<--- Score

92. How will you measure the results?
<--- Score

93. Is there a small-scale pilot for proposed improvement(s)? What conclusions were drawn from the outcomes of a pilot?
<--- Score

94. Is Supporting Project Control Stages documentation required?
<--- Score

95. Who will be using the results of the measurement
activities?
<--- Score

Add up total points for this section:
_____ = Total points for this section

Divided by: _____ (number of
statements answered) = _____
Average score for this section

Transfer your score to the Project
Control Stages Index at the beginning of
the Self-Assessment.

CRITERION #6: CONTROL:

INTENT: Implement the practical solution. Maintain the performance and correct possible complications.

In my belief, the answer to this question is clearly defined:

5 Strongly Agree

4 Agree

3 Neutral

2 Disagree

1 Strongly Disagree

1. How does your workforce performance management system support high-performance work and workforce engagement; consider workforce compensation, reward, recognition, and incentive practices; and reinforce a customer and business focus and achievement of your action plans?
<--- Score

2. What is your quality control system?
<--- Score

3. Implementation Planning- is a pilot needed to test the changes before a full roll out occurs?
<--- Score

4. How will the process owner and team be able to hold the gains?
<--- Score

5. Does a troubleshooting guide exist or is it needed?
<--- Score

6. What can you control?
<--- Score

7. Does the response plan contain a definite closed loop continual improvement scheme (e.g., plan-do-check-act)?
<--- Score

8. Is a response plan in place for when the input, process, or output measures indicate an 'out-of-control' condition?
<--- Score

9. Is there a recommended audit plan for routine surveillance inspections of Project Control Stages's gains?
<--- Score

10. How will the process owner verify improvement in present and future sigma levels, process capabilities?
<--- Score

11. Do the Project Control Stages decisions we make today help people and the planet tomorrow?
<--- Score

12. What is our theory of human motivation, and how does our compensation plan fit with that view?
<--- Score

13. Are new process steps, standards, and documentation ingrained into normal operations?
<--- Score

14. Whats the best design framework for Project Control Stages organization now that, in a post industrial-age if the top-down, command and control model is no longer relevant?
<--- Score

15. Are operating procedures consistent?
<--- Score

16. Were the planned controls working?
<--- Score

17. Is there a documented and implemented monitoring plan?
<--- Score

18. Who has control over resources?
<--- Score

19. How will new or emerging customer needs/requirements be checked/communicated to orient the process toward meeting the new specifications and continually reducing variation?

<--- Score

20. What other systems, operations, processes, and infrastructures (hiring practices, staffing, training, incentives/rewards, metrics/dashboards/scorecards, etc.) need updates, additions, changes, or deletions in order to facilitate knowledge transfer and improvements?
<--- Score

21. What should the next improvement project be that is related to Project Control Stages?
<--- Score

22. Are pertinent alerts monitored, analyzed and distributed to appropriate personnel?
<--- Score

23. What is your theory of human motivation, and how does your compensation plan fit with that view?
<--- Score

24. What quality tools were useful in the control phase?
<--- Score

25. What other areas of the group might benefit from the Project Control Stages team's improvements, knowledge, and learning?
<--- Score

26. Is reporting being used or needed?
<--- Score

27. How can we best use all of our knowledge repositories to enhance learning and sharing?

<--- Score

28. Does the Project Control Stages performance meet the customer's requirements?
<--- Score

29. What are the key elements of your Project Control Stages performance improvement system, including your evaluation, organizational learning, and innovation processes?
<--- Score

30. Does Project Control Stages appropriately measure and monitor risk?
<--- Score

31. Are documented procedures clear and easy to follow for the operators?
<--- Score

32. Is a response plan established and deployed?
<--- Score

33. Are suggested corrective/restorative actions indicated on the response plan for known causes to problems that might surface?
<--- Score

34. Will existing staff require re-training, for example, to learn new business processes?
<--- Score

35. What do we stand for--and what are we against?
<--- Score

36. What are the known security controls?
<--- Score

37. What should we measure to verify effectiveness gains?
<--- Score

38. Where do ideas that reach policy makers and planners as proposals for Project Control Stages strengthening and reform actually originate?
<--- Score

39. How likely is the current Project Control Stages plan to come in on schedule or on budget?
<--- Score

40. Are controls in place and consistently applied?
<--- Score

41. Is knowledge gained on process shared and institutionalized?
<--- Score

42. Who controls critical resources?
<--- Score

43. What are we attempting to measure/monitor?
<--- Score

44. Is there a standardized process?
<--- Score

45. Why is change control necessary?
<--- Score

46. How will the day-to-day responsibilities for

monitoring and continual improvement be transferred from the improvement team to the process owner?
<--- Score

47. What is the control/monitoring plan?
<--- Score

48. What should we measure to verify efficiency gains?
<--- Score

49. If there currently is no plan, will a plan be developed?
<--- Score

50. How do controls support value?
<--- Score

51. Is new knowledge gained imbedded in the response plan?
<--- Score

52. How might the group capture best practices and lessons learned so as to leverage improvements?
<--- Score

53. Is there a Project Control Stages Communication plan covering who needs to get what information when?
<--- Score

54. Do the decisions we make today help people and the planet tomorrow?
<--- Score

55. Do we monitor the Project Control Stages decisions made and fine tune them as they evolve?
<--- Score

56. Is there a control plan in place for sustaining improvements (short and long-term)?
<--- Score

57. Do you monitor the effectiveness of your Project Control Stages activities?
<--- Score

58. How do our controls stack up?
<--- Score

59. Will any special training be provided for results interpretation?
<--- Score

60. In the case of a Project Control Stages project, the criteria for the audit derive from implementation objectives. an audit of a Project Control Stages project involves assessing whether the recommendations outlined for implementation have been met. in other words, can we track that any Project Control Stages project is implemented as planned, and is it working?
<--- Score

61. Is there documentation that will support the successful operation of the improvement?
<--- Score

62. Who is the Project Control Stages process owner?
<--- Score

63. Against what alternative is success being measured?
<--- Score

64. Were the planned controls in place?
<--- Score

65. Has the improved process and its steps been standardized?
<--- Score

66. How do you encourage people to take control and responsibility?
<--- Score

67. Does job training on the documented procedures need to be part of the process team's education and training?
<--- Score

68. What are the critical parameters to watch?
<--- Score

69. Are there documented procedures?
<--- Score

70. How will input, process, and output variables be checked to detect for sub-optimal conditions?
<--- Score

71. Is there a transfer of ownership and knowledge to process owner and process team tasked with the responsibilities.
<--- Score

72. Have new or revised work instructions resulted?
<--- Score

73. What key inputs and outputs are being measured on an ongoing basis?
<--- Score

74. Who will be in control?
<--- Score

75. What are your results for key measures or indicators of the accomplishment of your Project Control Stages strategy and action plans, including building and strengthening core competencies?
<--- Score

76. How do we enable market innovation while controlling security and privacy?
<--- Score

77. How will report readings be checked to effectively monitor performance?
<--- Score

78. What is the recommended frequency of auditing?
<--- Score

Add up total points for this section:
_____ = Total points for this section

Divided by: _____ (number of statements answered) = _____
Average score for this section

Transfer your score to the Project

Control Stages Index at the beginning of
the Self-Assessment.

CRITERION #7: SUSTAIN:

INTENT: Retain the benefits.

In my belief, the answer to this question is clearly defined:

5 Strongly Agree

4 Agree

3 Neutral

2 Disagree

1 Strongly Disagree

1. How is it going to be used?
<--- Score

2. What external factors influence our success?
<--- Score

3. What will drive Project Control Stages change?
<--- Score

4. In a project to restructure Project Control Stages outcomes, which stakeholders would you involve?

<--- Score

5. How likely is it that a customer would recommend our company to a friend or colleague?
<--- Score

6. Why should we adopt a Project Control Stages framework?
<--- Score

7. Who else should we help?
<--- Score

8. What is value for money?
<--- Score

9. What resources are necessary?
<--- Score

10. Why don't our customers like us?
<--- Score

11. How Do We Know if We Are Successful?
<--- Score

12. What principles do we value?
<--- Score

13. Is a Project Control Stages Team Work effort in place?
<--- Score

14. What should we stop doing?
<--- Score

15. Instead of going to current contacts for new ideas,

what if you reconnected with dormant contacts--
the people you used to know? If you were going
reactivate a dormant tie, who would it be?
<--- Score

16. Who will be affected by the project?
<--- Score

17. What is an estimate?
<--- Score

18. Who will determine interim and final deadlines?
<--- Score

19. Are the criteria for selecting recommendations stated?
<--- Score

20. How do you govern and fulfill your societal responsibilities?
<--- Score

21. How do we foster innovation?
<--- Score

22. What is the timeline?
<--- Score

23. Are we / should we be Revolutionary or evolutionary?
<--- Score

24. What is our question?
<--- Score

25. What is the range of capabilities?
<--- Score

26. Who do we want our customers to become?
<--- Score

27. What will be the consequences to the stakeholder (financial, reputation etc) if Project Control Stages does not go ahead or fails to deliver the objectives?
<--- Score

28. Whose voice (department, ethnic group, women, older workers, etc) might you have missed hearing from in your company, and how might you amplify this voice to create positive momentum for your business?
<--- Score

29. How can we become more high-tech but still be high touch?
<--- Score

30. In retrospect, of the projects that we pulled the plug on, what percent do we wish had been allowed to keep going, and what percent do we wish had ended earlier?
<--- Score

31. If no one would ever find out about my accomplishments, how would I lead differently?
<--- Score

32. What are internal and external Project Control Stages relations?
<--- Score

33. What management system can we use to leverage the Project Control Stages experience, ideas, and concerns of the people closest to the work to be done?

<--- Score

34. What is your BATNA (best alternative to a negotiated agreement)?

<--- Score

35. What is our mission?

<--- Score

36. Am I failing differently each time?

<--- Score

37. Political -is anyone trying to undermine this project?

<--- Score

38. Is maximizing Project Control Stages protection the same as minimizing Project Control Stages loss?

<--- Score

39. What was the last experiment we ran?

<--- Score

40. Will I get fired?

<--- Score

41. Will it be accepted by users?

<--- Score

42. What potential megatrends could make our business model obsolete?

<--- Score

43. Who, on the executive team or the board, has spoken to a customer recently?
<--- Score

44. Is the impact that Project Control Stages has shown?
<--- Score

45. When is the Design Team appointed?
<--- Score

46. What information is critical to our organization that our executives are ignoring?
<--- Score

47. Do you keep 50% of your time unscheduled?
<--- Score

48. What do we do when new problems arise?
<--- Score

49. What are the Essentials of Internal Project Control Stages Management?
<--- Score

50. Who is the main stakeholder, with ultimate responsibility for driving Project Control Stages forward?
<--- Score

51. What are the challenges?
<--- Score

52. Are we paying enough attention to the partners

our company depends on to succeed?
<--- Score

53. Which criteria are used to determine which projects are going to be pursued or discarded?
<--- Score

54. What happens if you do not have enough funding?
<--- Score

55. Can we maintain our growth without detracting from the factors that have contributed to our success?
<--- Score

56. What are the usability implications of Project Control Stages actions?
<--- Score

57. Do we underestimate the customer's journey?
<--- Score

58. How do we keep the momentum going?
<--- Score

59. Where is our petri dish?
<--- Score

60. What current systems have to be understood and/or changed?
<--- Score

61. In the past year, what have you done (or could you have done) to increase the accurate perception of this company/brand as ethical and honest?

<--- Score

62. Do you see more potential in people than they do in themselves?
<--- Score

63. How do we accomplish our long range Project Control Stages goals?
<--- Score

64. How much information-buying is enough?
<--- Score

65. Are we relevant? Will we be relevant five years from now? Ten?
<--- Score

66. Who have we, as a company, historically been when we've been at our best?
<--- Score

67. What are the short and long-term Project Control Stages goals?
<--- Score

68. Where can we break convention?
<--- Score

69. What is our formula for success in Project Control Stages ?
<--- Score

70. What is a product life cycle?
<--- Score

71. If we weren't already in this business, would we

enter it today? And if not, what are we going to do about it?
<--- Score

72. How to deal with Project Control Stages Changes?
<--- Score

73. Is program in place as intended?
<--- Score

74. Are we changing as fast as the world around us?
<--- Score

75. Do we keep stake holders informed?
<--- Score

76. Who are the key stakeholders?
<--- Score

77. Use: How will they use the information?
<--- Score

78. What is Effective Project Control Stages?
<--- Score

79. What is the funding source for this project?
<--- Score

80. How do we ensure that implementations of Project Control Stages products are done in a way that ensures safety?
<--- Score

81. What is a GANTT Chart?
<--- Score

82. Who Uses What?
<--- Score

83. Schedule -can it be done in the given time?
<--- Score

84. What are the gaps in my knowledge and experience?
<--- Score

85. Why should people listen to you?
<--- Score

86. Who will be responsible for deciding whether Project Control Stages goes ahead or not after the initial investigations?
<--- Score

87. Legal and contractual - are we allowed to do this?
<--- Score

88. What are specific Project Control Stages Rules to follow?
<--- Score

89. If we got kicked out and the board brought in a new CEO, what would he do?
<--- Score

90. What stupid rule would we most like to kill?
<--- Score

91. Have new benefits been realized?
<--- Score

92. What sources do you use to gather information for a Project Control Stages study?
<--- Score

93. Do we have enough freaky customers in our portfolio pushing us to the limit day in and day out?
<--- Score

94. How is it justified?
<--- Score

95. Did my employees make progress today?
<--- Score

96. When information truly is ubiquitous, when reach and connectivity are completely global, when computing resources are infinite, and when a whole new set of impossibilities are not only possible, but happening, what will that do to our business?
<--- Score

97. Are there Project Control Stages Models?
<--- Score

98. Is there any existing Project Control Stages governance structure?
<--- Score

99. If I had to leave my organization for a year and the only communication I could have with employees was a single paragraph, what would I write?
<--- Score

100. What is the project for?
<--- Score

101. What are the business goals Project Control Stages is aiming to achieve?
<--- Score

102. What kind of crime could a potential new hire have committed that would not only not disqualify him/her from being hired by our organization, but would actually indicate that he/she might be a particularly good fit?
<--- Score

103. How will we know when our strategy has been successful?
<--- Score

104. How do we engage the workforce, in addition to satisfying them?
<--- Score

105. You may have created your customer policies at a time when you lacked resources, technology wasn't up-to-snuff, or low service levels were the industry norm. Have those circumstances changed?
<--- Score

106. What is the purpose of Project Control Stages in relation to the mission?
<--- Score

107. Have highly satisfied employees?
<--- Score

108. Do we think we know, or do we know we know ?
<--- Score

109. How long will it take to change?

<--- Score

110. Do we say no to customers for no reason?

<--- Score

111. Do you have an implicit bias for capital investments over people investments?

<--- Score

112. What threat is Project Control Stages addressing?

<--- Score

113. What is our competitive advantage?

<--- Score

114. Why are Project Control Stages skills important?

<--- Score

115. If our customer were my grandmother, would I tell her to buy what we're selling?

<--- Score

116. Who are you going to put out of business, and why?

<--- Score

117. Who is doing what for whom?

<--- Score

118. What am I trying to prove to myself, and how might it be hijacking my life and business success?

<--- Score

119. What trouble can we get into?

<--- Score

120. Have benefits been optimized with all key stakeholders?
<--- Score

121. Who is going to care?
<--- Score

122. What trophy do we want on our mantle?
<--- Score

123. What did we miss in the interview for the worst hire we ever made?
<--- Score

124. How much contingency will be available in the budget?
<--- Score

125. Who uses our product in ways we never expected?
<--- Score

126. What are your key business, operational, societal responsibility, and human resource strategic challenges and advantages?
<--- Score

127. Has implementation been effective in reaching specified objectives?
<--- Score

128. What is performance excellence?
<--- Score

129. What are the critical success factors?
<--- Score

130. How will we build a 100-year startup?
<--- Score

131. Among our stronger employees, how many
see themselves at the company in three years? How
many would leave for a 10 percent raise from another
company?
<--- Score

132. Who are our customers?
<--- Score

133. Who do we think the world wants us to be?
<--- Score

134. What is an unauthorized commitment?
<--- Score

135. Have totally satisfied customers?
<--- Score

**136. If you were responsible for initiating and
implementing major changes in your organization,
what steps might you take to ensure acceptance of
those changes?**
<--- Score

**137. How do we make it meaningful in connecting
Project Control Stages with what users do day-to-
day?**
<--- Score

138. Which individuals, teams or departments will be

involved in Project Control Stages?
<--- Score

139. What knowledge, skills and characteristics mark a good Project Control Stages project manager?
<--- Score

140. How can you negotiate Project Control Stages successfully with a stubborn boss, an irate client, or a deceitful coworker?
<--- Score

141. If there were zero limitations, what would we do differently?
<--- Score

142. Who will manage the integration of tools?
<--- Score

143. How will we know if we have been successful?
<--- Score

144. What is Tricky About This?
<--- Score

145. How is business? Why?
<--- Score

146. Do Project Control Stages rules make a reasonable demand on a users capabilities?
<--- Score

147. What are all of our Project Control Stages domains and what do they do?
<--- Score

148. How do you determine the key elements that affect Project Control Stages workforce satisfaction? how are these elements determined for different workforce groups and segments?
<--- Score

149. But does it really, really work?
<--- Score

150. What is the mission of the organization?
<--- Score

151. Do we have the right capabilities and capacities?
<--- Score

152. Are you satisfied with your current role? If not, what is missing from it?
<--- Score

153. Which models, tools and techniques are necessary?
<--- Score

154. How Do We Create Buy-in?
<--- Score

155. What is the estimated value of the project?
<--- Score

156. What happens when a new employee joins the organization?
<--- Score

157. If we do not follow, then how to lead?

<--- Score

158. Are we making progress?
<--- Score

159. What is the craziest thing we can do?
<--- Score

160. Are the activities sustainable?
<--- Score

161. What is it like to work for me?
<--- Score

162. In what ways are Project Control Stages vendors and us interacting to ensure safe and effective use?
<--- Score

163. What are strategies for increasing support and reducing opposition?
<--- Score

164. How does Project Control Stages integrate with other stakeholder initiatives?
<--- Score

165. How do senior leaders deploy your organizations vision and values through your leadership system, to the workforce, to key suppliers and partners, and to customers and other stakeholders, as appropriate?
<--- Score

166. What is the timeline for the project?
<--- Score

167. How will we insure seamless interoperability of Project Control Stages moving forward?

<--- Score

168. Are assumptions made in Project Control Stages stated explicitly?

<--- Score

169. Where Do Changes Come From?

<--- Score

170. How do we foster the skills, knowledge, talents, attributes, and characteristics we want to have?

<--- Score

171. Who will use it?

<--- Score

172. What is a feasible sequencing of reform initiatives over time?

<--- Score

173. How important is Project Control Stages to the user organizations mission?

<--- Score

174. Whom does it serve?

<--- Score

175. How do we know when we are finished?

<--- Score

176. How do we maintain Project Control Stages's Integrity?

<--- Score

177. What are your most important goals for the strategic Project Control Stages objectives?
<--- Score

178. Where is your organization on the performance excellence continuum?
<--- Score

179. Do your leaders set clear a direction that is aligned with the vision, mission, and values and is cascaded throughout the organization with measurable goals?
<--- Score

180. Who sets the Project Control Stages standards?
<--- Score

181. Is there a lack of internal resources to do this work?
<--- Score

182. How would our PR, marketing, and social media change if we did not use outside agencies?
<--- Score

183. Is Project Control Stages dependent on the successful delivery of a current project?
<--- Score

184. Do you have any supplemental information to add to this checklist?
<--- Score

185. How much money have we spent?

<--- Score

186. Would you rather sell to knowledgeable and informed customers or to uninformed customers?
<--- Score

187. Are there any disadvantages to implementing Project Control Stages? There might be some that are less obvious?
<--- Score

188. What is the overall business strategy?

<--- Score

189. What have we done to protect our business from competitive encroachment?
<--- Score

190. How are conflicts dealt with?

<--- Score

191. How are we doing compared to our industry?

<--- Score

192. Do I know what I'm doing? And who do I call if I don't?
<--- Score

193. Do you have a vision statement?

<--- Score

194. To whom do you add value?
<--- Score

195. What are our long-range and short-range

goals?
<--- Score

196. Ask yourself: how would we do this work if we only had one staff member to do it?
<--- Score

197. Whom among your colleagues do you trust, and for what?
<--- Score

198. What are the success criteria that will indicate that Project Control Stages objectives have been met and the benefits delivered?
<--- Score

199. What counts that we are not counting?
<--- Score

200. Has the investment re-baselined during the past fiscal year?
<--- Score

201. What may be the consequences for the performance of an organization if all stakeholders are not consulted regarding Project Control Stages?
<--- Score

202. What are the goals of the program?
<--- Score

203. Think about the kind of project structure that would be appropriate for your Project Control Stages project. should it be formal and complex, or can it be less formal and relatively simple?

<--- Score

204. Are new benefits received and understood?
<--- Score

205. Do we have the right people on the bus?
<--- Score

206. How do we manage Project Control Stages Knowledge Management (KM)?
<--- Score

207. What are the long-term Project Control Stages goals?
<--- Score

208. Are the assumptions believable and achievable?
<--- Score

209. If you had to rebuild your organization without any traditional competitive advantages (i.e., no killer a technology, promising research, innovative product/service delivery model, etc.), how would your people have to approach their work and collaborate together in order to create the necessary conditions for success?
<--- Score

210. How do we go about Securing Project Control Stages?
<--- Score

211. How can we become the company that would put us out of business?
<--- Score

212. What are we challenging, in the sense that Mac challenged the PC or Dove tackled the Beauty Myth?
<--- Score

213. How do I stay inspired?
<--- Score

214. Who is responsible for ensuring appropriate resources (time, people and money) are allocated to Project Control Stages?
<--- Score

215. Marketing budgets are tighter, consumers are more skeptical, and social media has changed forever the way we talk about Project Control Stages. How do we gain traction?
<--- Score

216. What would have to be true for the option on the table to be the best possible choice?
<--- Score

217. What are your organizations work systems?
<--- Score

218. Who is On the Team?
<--- Score

219. How many changes are we making?
<--- Score

220. What are the rules and assumptions my industry operates under? What if the opposite were true?
<--- Score

221. How will we ensure we get what we expected?
<--- Score

222. How can we incorporate support to ensure safe and effective use of Project Control Stages into the services that we provide?
<--- Score

223. How do senior leaders set organizational vision and values?
<--- Score

224. Is our strategy driving our strategy? Or is the way in which we allocate resources driving our strategy?
<--- Score

225. What one word do we want to own in the minds of our customers, employees, and partners?
<--- Score

226. What does your signature ensure?
<--- Score

227. What business benefits will Project Control Stages goals deliver if achieved?
<--- Score

228. Who is responsible for errors?
<--- Score

229. What is our Project Control Stages Strategy?
<--- Score

230. Who are four people whose careers I've enhanced?
<--- Score

231. How do you listen to customers to obtain actionable information?
<--- Score

232. Will there be any necessary staff changes (redundancies or new hires)?
<--- Score

233. What happens at this company when people fail?
<--- Score

234. How do we provide a safe environment -physically and emotionally?
<--- Score

235. Were lessons learned captured and communicated?
<--- Score

236. Are we making progress (as leaders)?
<--- Score

237. How much does Project Control Stages help?
<--- Score

238. Is the Project Control Stages organization completing tasks effectively and efficiently?
<--- Score

239. Is it economical; do we have the time and money?
<--- Score

240. What would I recommend my friend do if he were facing this dilemma?

<--- Score

241. Is there any reason to believe the opposite of my current belief?
<--- Score

242. Are we making progress? and are we making progress as Project Control Stages leaders?
<--- Score

243. What is a good product?
<--- Score

244. We picked a method, now what?
<--- Score

245. Which Project Control Stages goals are the most important?
<--- Score

246. How was the program set-up initiated?
<--- Score

247. If our company went out of business tomorrow, would anyone who doesn't get a paycheck here care?
<--- Score

248. What new services of functionality will be implemented next with Project Control Stages ?
<--- Score

249. How do we Lead with Project Control Stages in Mind?
<--- Score

250. Think of your Project Control Stages project.

what are the main functions?

<--- Score

251. Operational - will it work?

<--- Score

252. Who will provide the final approval of Project Control Stages deliverables?

<--- Score

253. Which functions and people interact with the supplier and or customer?

<--- Score

254. How do we know how we are doing?

<--- Score

255. What is something you believe that nearly no one agrees with you on?

<--- Score

256. What role does communication play in the success or failure of a Project Control Stages project?

<--- Score

257. How will you know that the Project Control Stages project has been successful?

<--- Score

258. How to Secure Project Control Stages?

<--- Score

Add up total points for this section:
_ _ _ _ _ = Total points for this section

Divided by: _____ (number of
statements answered) = _____
Average score for this section

Transfer your score to the Project
Control Stages Index at the beginning of
the Self-Assessment.

Project Control Stages and Managing Projects, Criteria for Project Managers:

1.0 Initiating Process Group: Project Control Stages

1. What will be the pressing issues of tomorrow?

2. Were decisions made in a timely manner?

3. How will you do it?

4. How well did the chosen processes fit the needs of the Project Control Stages project?

5. Do you understand the quality and control criteria that must be achieved for successful Project Control Stages project completion?

6. Are the changes in your Project Control Stages project being formally requested, analyzed, and approved by the appropriate decision makers?

7. The Project Control Stages project you are managing has nine stakeholders. How many channel of communications are there between corresponding stakeholders?

8. How do you help others satisfy needs?

9. Do you know the roles & responsibilities required for this Project Control Stages project?

10. The Project Control Stages project managers have maximum authority in which type of organization?

11. Who is involved in each phase?

12. During which stage of Risk planning are risks prioritized based on probability and impact?

13. Are you just doing busywork to pass the time?

14. The process to Manage Stakeholders is part of which process group?

15. Are the Project Control Stages project team and stakeholders meeting regularly and using a meeting agenda and taking notes to accurately document what is being covered and what happened in the weekly meetings?

16. How to control and approve each phase?

17. What technical work to do in each phase?

18. Are you certain deliverables are properly completed and meet quality standards?

19. During which stage of Risk planning are modeling techniques used to determine overall effects of risks on Project Control Stages project objectives for high probability, high impact risks?

20. Realistic - are the desired results expressed in a way that the team will be motivated and believe that the required level of involvement will be obtained?

1.1 Project Charter: Project Control Stages

21. Name and describe the elements that deal with providing the detail?

22. Fit with other Products Compliments – Cannibalizes?

23. What ideas do you have for initial tests of change (PDSA cycles)?

24. Why use a Project Control Stages project charter?

25. What are the constraints?

26. How high should you set your goals?

27. Why executive support?

28. What are the deliverables?

29. How are Project Control Stages projects different from operations?

30. What are the assumptions?

31. Why is a Project Control Stages project Charter used?

32. How much?

33. What is the most common tool for helping define

the detail?

34. When is a charter needed?

35. Customer: who are you doing the Project Control Stages project for?

36. Project Control Stages project background: what is the primary motivation for this Project Control Stages project?

37. What are you striving to accomplish (measurable goal(s))?

38. What are some examples of a business case?

39. Are there special technology requirements?

40. Why Outsource?

1.2 Stakeholder Register: Project Control Stages

41. What are the major Project Control Stages project milestones requiring communications or providing communications opportunities?

42. What is the power of the stakeholder?

43. Is your organization ready for change?

44. What opportunities exist to provide communications?

45. Who are the stakeholders?

46. What & Why?

47. How much influence do they have on the Project Control Stages project?

48. How should employers make voices heard?

49. How will reports be created?

50. Who is managing stakeholder engagement?

51. How big is the gap?

52. Who wants to talk about Security?

1.3 Stakeholder Analysis Matrix: Project Control Stages

53. Effects on core activities, distraction?

54. Do any safeguard policies apply to the Project Control Stages project?

55. Which conditions out of the control of the management are crucial for the achievement of the immediate objective?

56. What obstacles does your organization face?

57. Does the stakeholder want to be involved or merely need to be informed about the Project Control Stages project and its process?

58. Sustainable financial backing?

59. Competitive advantages?

60. Market developments?

61. Advantages of proposition?

62. Are you working on the right risks?

63. What is your Risk Management?

64. Resources, assets, people?

65. Participatory approach: how will key stakeholders

participate in the Project Control Stages project?

66. Market demand?

67. Loss of key staff?

68. How to involve media?

69. What makes a person a stakeholder?

70. Guiding question: what is the issue at stake?

71. Are there people who ise voices or interests in the issue may not be heard?

72. Vulnerable groups; who are the vulnerable groups that might be affected by the Project Control Stages project?

2.0 Planning Process Group: Project Control Stages

73. What factors are contributing to progress or delay in the achievement of products and results?

74. Are there efficient coordination mechanisms to avoid overloading the counterparts, participating stakeholders?

75. What types of differentiated effects are resulting from the Project Control Stages project and to what extent?

76. What good practices or successful experiences or transferable examples have been identified?

77. To what extent have public/private national resources and/or counterparts been mobilized to contribute to the programs objective and produce results and impacts?

78. What is the difference between the early schedule and late schedule?

79. To what extent has a PMO contributed to raising the quality of the design of the Project Control Stages project?

80. What are the different approaches to building the WBS?

81. Who are the Project Control Stages project

stakeholders?

82. Have more efficient (sensitive) and appropriate measures been adopted to respond to the political and socio-cultural problems identified?

83. How should needs be met?

84. What input will you be required to provide the Project Control Stages project team?

85. Does it make any difference if you are successful?

86. What do you need to do?

87. Did the program design/ implementation strategy adequately address the planning stage necessary to set up structures, hire staff etc.?

88. You are creating your WBS and find that you keep decomposing tasks into smaller and smaller units. How can you tell when you are done?

89. Explanation: is what the Project Control Stages project intents to solve a hard question?

90. How many days can task X be late in starting without affecting the Project Control Stages project completion date?

91. In what ways can the governance of the Project Control Stages project be improved so that it has greater likelihood of achieving future sustainability?

92. What is the critical path for this Project Control Stages project, and what is the duration of the critical

path?

2.1 Project Management Plan: Project Control Stages

93. How do you organize the costs in the Project Control Stages project management plan?

94. Where does all this information come from?

95. Is the budget realistic?

96. Is the engineering content at a feasibility level-of-detail, and is it sufficiently complete, to provide an adequate basis for the baseline cost estimate?

97. What went right?

98. Are alternatives safe, functional, constructible, economical, reasonable and sustainable?

99. How do you manage integration?

100. How do you manage time?

101. What goes into your Project Control Stages project Charter?

102. If the Project Control Stages project management plan is a comprehensive document that guides you in Project Control Stages project execution and control, then what should it NOT contain?

103. Development trends and opportunities. What if the positive direction and vision of your organization

causes expected trends to change?

104. Was the peer (technical) review of the cost estimates duly coordinated with the cost estimate center of expertise and addressed in the review documentation and certification?

105. Is there anything you would now do differently on your Project Control Stages project based on past experience?

106. Are cost risk analysis methods applied to develop contingencies for the estimated total Project Control Stages project costs?

107. Has the selected plan been formulated using cost effectiveness and incremental analysis techniques?

108. Do there need to be organizational changes?

109. Does the implementation plan have an appropriate division of responsibilities?

110. What are the training needs?

111. What is the business need?

112. What does management expect of PMs?

2.2 Scope Management Plan: Project Control Stages

113. Does the quality assurance process provide objective verification of adherence to applicable standards, procedures & requirements?

114. Have the key elements of a coherent Project Control Stages project management strategy been established?

115. What strengths do you have?

116. Without-plan conditions?

117. Are the schedule estimates reasonable given the Project Control Stages project?

118. Are calculations and results of analyzes essentially correct?

119. Has stakeholder analysis been conducted, assessing influence on the Project Control Stages project and authority levels?

120. Have activity relationships and interdependencies within tasks been adequately identified?

121. Are Project Control Stages project team members involved in detailed estimating and scheduling?

122. Organizational unit (e.g., department, team, or

person) who will accept responsibility for satisfactory completion of the item?

123. Deliverables -are the deliverables tangible and verifiable?

124. How relevant is this attribute to this Project Control Stages project or audit?

125. What are the Quality Assurance overheads?

126. Is there an onboarding process in place?

127. Are cause and effect determined for risks when they occur?

128. Has a resource management plan been created?

129. Has a proper Project Control Stages project work location been established that will allow the team to work together with user personnel?

130. Are the appropriate IT resources adequate to meet planned commitments?

2.3 Requirements Management Plan: Project Control Stages

131. Did you provide clear and concise specifications?

132. Who is responsible for quantifying the Project Control Stages project requirements?

133. Did you get proper approvals?

134. How often will the reporting occur?

135. Which hardware or software, related to, or as outcome of the Project Control Stages project is new to your organization?

136. Will you perform a Requirements Risk assessment and develop a plan to deal with risks?

137. Do you have price sheets and a methodology for determining the total proposal cost?

138. How will the requirements become prioritized?

139. Who has the authority to reject Project Control Stages project requirements?

140. Is the change control process documented?

141. Who will do the reporting and to whom will reports be delivered?

142. What information regarding the Project Control

Stages project requirements will be reported?

143. Will you have access to stakeholders when you need them?

144. How will the information be distributed?

145. Do you understand the role that each stakeholder will play in the requirements process?

146. What is the earliest finish date for this Project Control Stages project if it is scheduled to start on ...?

147. Who will perform the analysis?

148. Define the help desk model. who will take full responsibility?

149. Describe the process for rejecting the Project Control Stages project requirements. Who has the authority to reject Project Control Stages project requirements?

2.4 Requirements Documentation: Project Control Stages

150. What images does it conjure?

151. What variations exist for a process?

152. Can you check system requirements?

153. How do you get the user to tell you what they want?

154. What are the potential disadvantages/ advantages?

155. How linear / iterative is your Requirements Gathering process (or will it be)?

156. Does your organization restrict technical alternatives?

157. Who is interacting with the system?

158. Who provides requirements?

159. Do technical resources exist?

160. Are there legal issues?

161. Has requirements gathering uncovered information that would necessitate changes?

162. How will requirements be documented and who

signs off on them?

163. Where are business rules being captured?

164. Is the origin of the requirement clearly stated?

165. Are there any requirements conflicts?

166. Can the requirement be changed without a large impact on other requirements?

167. What facilities must be supported by the system?

168. What is the risk associated with the technology?

169. What can tools do for us?

2.5 Requirements Traceability Matrix: Project Control Stages

170. Why use a WBS?

171. Describe the process for approving requirements so they can be added to the traceability matrix and Project Control Stages project work can be performed. Will the Project Control Stages project requirements become approved in writing?

172. What percentage of Project Control Stages projects are producing traceability matrices between requirements and other work products?

173. How will it affect the stakeholders personally in their career?

174. Will you use a Requirements Traceability Matrix?

175. Do you have a clear understanding of all subcontracts in place?

176. How do you manage scope?

177. What is the WBS?

178. How small is small enough?

179. Why do you manage scope?

180. What are the chronologies, contingencies, consequences, criteria?

181. Is there a requirements traceability process in place?

2.6 Project Scope Statement: Project Control Stages

182. Are the meetings set up to have assigned note takers that will add action/issues to the issue list?

183. What should you drop in order to add something new?

184. Is the quality function identified and assigned?

185. What are the major deliverables of the Project Control Stages project?

186. Will the risk documents be filed?

187. How often will scope changes be reviewed?

188. Is the Project Control Stages project organization documented and on file?

189. Have you been able to easily identify success criteria and create objective measurements for each of the Project Control Stages project scopes goal statements?

190. Is there a process (test plans, inspections, reviews) defined for verifying outputs for each task?

191. Write a brief purpose statement for this Project Control Stages project. Include a business justification statement. What is the product of this Project Control Stages project?

192. Are there specific processes you will use to evaluate and approve/reject changes?

193. Change management vs. change leadership - what is the difference?

194. How will you verify the accuracy of the work of the Project Control Stages project, and what constitutes acceptance of the deliverables?

195. Elements of scope management that deal with concept development ?

196. Is there a baseline plan against which to measure progress?

197. What went wrong?

198. Once its defined, what is the stability of the Project Control Stages project scope?

199. Is the plan under configuration management?

2.7 Assumption and Constraint Log: Project Control Stages

200. How relevant is this attribute to this Project Control Stages project or audit?

201. How can you prevent/fix violations?

202. Is the process working, and people are not executing in compliance of the process?

203. Should factors be unpredictable over time?

204. Does the document/deliverable meet general requirements (for example, statement of work) for all deliverables?

205. Are there unnecessary steps that are creating bottlenecks and/or causing people to wait?

206. Contradictory information between different documents?

207. If appropriate, is the deliverable content consistent with current Project Control Stages project documents and in compliance with the Document Management Plan?

208. Is the amount of effort justified by the anticipated value of forming a new process?

209. Does the traceability documentation describe the tool and/or mechanism to be used to capture

traceability throughout the life cycle?

210. Are you meeting your customers expectations consistently?

211. Do you know what your customers expectations are regarding this process?

212. Is the current scope of the Project Control Stages project substantially different than that originally defined in the approved Project Control Stages project plan?

213. Are requirements management tracking tools and procedures in place?

214. Is the definition of the Project Control Stages project scope clear; what needs to be accomplished?

215. What worked well?

216. Are funding and staffing resource estimates sufficiently detailed and documented for use in planning and tracking the Project Control Stages project?

217. Does the system design reflect the requirements?

218. Are there processes defining how software will be developed including development methods, overall timeline for development, software product standards, and traceability?

219. What threats might prevent you from getting there?

2.8 Work Breakdown Structure: Project Control Stages

220. Why is it useful?

221. Where does it take place?

222. Why would you develop a Work Breakdown Structure?

223. When do you stop?

224. Is it a change in scope?

225. When would you develop a Work Breakdown Structure?

226. Is the work breakdown structure (wbs) defined and is the scope of the Project Control Stages project clear with assigned deliverable owners?

227. What is the probability of completing the Project Control Stages project in less that xx days?

228. Who has to do it?

229. What has to be done?

230. Can you make it?

231. How many levels?

232. Do you need another level?

233. How big is a work-package?

234. How will you and your Project Control Stages project team define the Project Control Stages projects scope and work breakdown structure?

235. How much detail?

236. Is it still viable?

237. What is the probability that the Project Control Stages project duration will exceed xx weeks?

238. How far down?

239. When does it have to be done?

2.9 WBS Dictionary: Project Control Stages

240. Are retroactive changes to BCWS and BCWP prohibited except for correction of errors or for normal accounting adjustments?

241. Are the latest revised estimates of costs at completion compared with the established budgets at appropriate levels and causes of variances identified?

242. Should you include sub-activities?

243. Changes in the direct base to which overhead costs are allocated?

244. Are current budgets resulting from changes to the authorized work and/or internal replanning, reconcilable to original budgets for specified reporting items?

245. Are the procedures for identifying indirect costs to incurring organizations, indirect cost pools, and allocating the costs from the pools to the contracts formally documented?

246. Where engineering standards or other internal work measurement systems are used, is there a formal relationship between corresponding values and work package budgets?

247. Incurrence of actual indirect costs in excess of

budgets, by element of expense?

248. Are estimates of costs at completion utilized in determining contract funding requirements and reporting them?

249. Are records maintained to show how management reserves are used?

250. Are estimates of costs at completion generated in a rational, consistent manner?

251. Detailed schedules which support control account and work package start and completion dates/events?

252. Are overhead costs budgets established on a basis consistent with anticipated direct business base?

253. Does the contractors system identify work accomplishment against the schedule plan?

254. Major functional areas of contract effort?

255. Does the contractors system description or procedures require that the performance measurement baseline plus management reserve equal the contract budget base?

256. Evaluate the performance of operating organizations?

257. Are work packages assigned to performing organizations?

258. Is each control account assigned to a single organizational element directly responsible for the work and identifiable to a single element of the CWBS?

2.10 Schedule Management Plan: Project Control Stages

259. Are enough systems & user personnel assigned to the Project Control Stages project?

260. Are all resource assumptions documented?

261. Are staff skills known and available for each task?

262. Goal: is the schedule feasible and at what cost?

263. Are all payments made according to the contract(s)?

264. Are adequate resources provided for the quality assurance function?

265. Does the Project Control Stages project have a Quality Culture?

266. Is there a formal set of procedures supporting Stakeholder Management?

267. Are all activities logically sequenced?

268. How are Project Control Stages projects different from operations?

269. Are corrective actions and variances reported?

270. Has the scope management document been updated and distributed to help prevent scope creep?

271. Cost / benefit analysis?

272. Are updated Project Control Stages project time & resource estimates reasonable based on the current Project Control Stages project stage?

273. Who is responsible for estimating the activity resources?

274. What does a valid Schedule look like?

275. Why conduct schedule analysis?

276. Are written status reports provided on a designated frequent basis?

277. Has a Project Control Stages project Communications Plan been developed?

278. Are risk oriented checklists used during risk identification?

2.11 Activity List: Project Control Stages

279. How detailed should a Project Control Stages project get?

280. When will the work be performed?

281. In what sequence?

282. What are you counting on?

283. When do the individual activities need to start and finish?

284. How can the Project Control Stages project be displayed graphically to better visualize the activities?

285. How do you determine the late start (LS) for each activity?

286. Can you determine the activity that must finish, before this activity can start?

287. Is infrastructure setup part of your Project Control Stages project?

288. What will be performed?

289. Where will it be performed?

290. How will it be performed?

291. How much slack is available in the Project Control Stages project?

292. How should ongoing costs be monitored to try to keep the Project Control Stages project within budget?

293. Are the required resources available or need to be acquired?

294. What went well?

295. Is there anything planned that does not need to be here?

296. What is the LF and LS for each activity?

2.12 Activity Attributes: Project Control Stages

297. What is missing?

298. What activity do you think you should spend the most time on?

299. How many days do you need to complete the work scope with a limit of X number of resources?

300. Can more resources be added?

301. Activity: what is In the Bag?

302. How difficult will it be to do specific activities on this Project Control Stages project?

303. Do you feel very comfortable with your prediction?

304. What conclusions/generalizations can you draw from this?

305. What is the general pattern here?

306. Activity: what is Missing?

307. Can you re-assign any activities to another resource to resolve an over-allocation?

308. Time for overtime?

309. Resources to accomplish the work?

310. Which method produces the more accurate cost assignment?

311. How else could the items be grouped?

312. Has management defined a definite timeframe for the turnaround or Project Control Stages project window?

313. Why?

2.13 Milestone List: Project Control Stages

314. Political effects?

315. What specific improvements did you make to the Project Control Stages project proposal since the previous time?

316. What would happen if a delivery of material was one week late?

317. Milestone pages should display the UserID of the person who added the milestone. Does a report or query exist that provides this audit information?

318. Identify critical paths (one or more) and which activities are on the critical path?

319. Can you derive how soon can the whole Project Control Stages project finish?

320. Gaps in capabilities?

321. Insurmountable weaknesses?

322. Describe the concept of the technology, product or service that will be or has been developed. How will it be used?

323. How soon can the activity finish?

324. What is your organizations history in doing

similar activities?

325. How late can each activity be finished and started?

326. Global influences?

327. New USPs?

328. Describe your organizations strengths and core competencies. What factors will make your organization succeed?

329. Marketing - reach, distribution, awareness?

330. How late can the activity start?

331. Who will manage the Project Control Stages project on a day-to-day basis?

2.14 Network Diagram: Project Control Stages

332. What controls the start and finish of a job?

333. What activities must follow this activity?

334. How difficult will it be to do specific activities on this Project Control Stages project?

335. Where do schedules come from?

336. What can be done concurrently?

337. How confident can you be in your milestone dates and the delivery date?

338. What are the tools?

339. If x is long, what would be the completion time if you break x into two parallel parts of y weeks and z weeks?

340. What are the Major Administrative Issues?

341. What activity must be completed immediately before this activity can start?

342. If the Project Control Stages project network diagram cannot change and you have extra personnel resources, what is the BEST thing to do?

343. What is the probability of completing the Project

Control Stages project in less that xx days?

344. Review the logical flow of the network diagram. Take a look at which activities you have first and then sequence the activities. Do they make sense?

345. What is the lowest cost to complete this Project Control Stages project in xx weeks?

346. Exercise: what is the probability that the Project Control Stages project duration will exceed xx weeks?

347. What to do and When?

348. Are the gantt chart and/or network diagram updated periodically and used to assess the overall Project Control Stages project timetable?

349. Will crashing x weeks return more in benefits than it costs?

350. What is the completion time?

351. Which type of network diagram allows you to depict four types of dependencies?

2.15 Activity Resource Requirements: Project Control Stages

352. Organizational Applicability?

353. Do you use tools like decomposition and rolling-wave planning to produce the activity list and other outputs?

354. When does monitoring begin?

355. What are constraints that you might find during the Human Resource Planning process?

356. Are there unresolved issues that need to be addressed?

357. Why do you do that?

358. Other support in specific areas?

359. Anything else?

360. What is the Work Plan Standard?

361. How do you handle petty cash?

362. How many signatures do you require on a check and does this match what is in your policy and procedures?

363. Which logical relationship does the PDM use most often?

2.16 Resource Breakdown Structure: Project Control Stages

364. Why do you do it?

365. What is the primary purpose of the human resource plan?

366. Why time management?

367. What is the number one predictor of a groups productivity?

368. When do they need the information?

369. How should the information be delivered?

370. Why is this important?

371. Any changes from stakeholders?

372. What are the requirements for resource data?

373. Which resources should be in the resource pool?

374. How can this help you with team building?

375. Changes based on input from stakeholders?

376. Goals for the Project Control Stages project. What is each stakeholders desired outcome for the Project Control Stages project?

377. What is the purpose of assigning and documenting responsibility?

378. What defines a successful Project Control Stages project?

379. The list could probably go on, but, the thing that you would most like to know is, How long & How much?

380. Who will use the system?

2.17 Activity Duration Estimates: Project Control Stages

381. Do you think Project Control Stages project managers of large information technology Project Control Stages projects need strong technical skills?

382. Are Project Control Stages project results verified and Project Control Stages project documents archived?

383. How have experts such as Deming, Juran, Crosby, and Taguchi affected the quality movement and todays use of Six Sigma?

384. How do you enter durations, link tasks, and view critical path information?

385. What are the largest companies that provide information technology outsourcing services?

386. Are procedures followed to ensure information is available to stakeholders in a timely manner?

387. Is the Project Control Stages project performing better or worse than planned?

388. Project Control Stages project has three critical paths. Which BEST describes how this affects the Project Control Stages project?

389. On which process should team members spend the most time?

390. How is the Project Control Stages project doing?

391. What is wrong with this scenario?

392. Is training acquired to enhance the skills, knowledge and capabilities of the Project Control Stages project team?

393. Are many products available?

394. Are processes defined to monitor Project Control Stages project cost and schedule variances?

395. What is the difference between using brainstorming and the Delphi technique for risk identification?

396. How can others help Project Control Stages project managers understand your organizational context for Project Control Stages projects?

397. What tasks can take place concurrently?

398. Do stakeholders follow a procedure for formally accepting the Project Control Stages project scope?

399. Calculate the expected duration for an activity that has a most likely time of 3, a pessimistic time of 10, and a optimiztic time of 2?

400. What does it mean to take a systems view of a Project Control Stages project?

2.18 Duration Estimating Worksheet: Project Control Stages

401. When does your organization expect to be able to complete it?

402. Is this operation cost effective?

403. What work will be included in the Project Control Stages project?

404. Define the work as completely as possible. What work will be included in the Project Control Stages project?

405. What is next?

406. What questions do you have?

407. What is cost and Project Control Stages project cost management?

408. When, then?

409. How should ongoing costs be monitored to try to keep the Project Control Stages project within budget?

410. Is the Project Control Stages project responsive to community need?

411. What is an Average Project Control Stages project?

412. Done before proceeding with this activity or what can be done concurrently?

413. Why estimate time and cost?

414. Small or large Project Control Stages project?

415. Can the Project Control Stages project be constructed as planned?

416. What is your role?

417. Science = process: remember the scientific method?

418. What info is needed?

419. Value pocket identification & quantification what are value pockets?

2.19 Project Schedule: Project Control Stages

420. How do you use schedules?

421. Was the Project Control Stages project schedule reviewed by all stakeholders and formally accepted?

422. Are procedures defined by which the Project Control Stages project schedule may be changed?

423. How can you fix it?

424. Why do you think schedule issues often cause the most conflicts on Project Control Stages projects?

425. Should you have a test for each code module?

426. How effectively were issues able to be resolved without impacting the Project Control Stages project Schedule or Budget?

427. Are the original Project Control Stages project schedule and budget realistic?

428. What is Project Control Stages project management?

429. What does that mean?

430. Is Project Control Stages project work proceeding in accordance with the original Project Control Stages project schedule?

431. What is risk management?

432. Your best shot for providing estimations how complex/how much work does the activity require?

433. How does a Project Control Stages project get to be a year late ?

434. How can you address that situation?

435. If there are any qualifying green components to this Project Control Stages project, what portion of the total Project Control Stages project cost is green?

436. Your Project Control Stages project management plan results in a Project Control Stages project schedule that is too long. If the Project Control Stages project network diagram cannot change and you have extra personnel resources, what is the BEST thing to do?

2.20 Cost Management Plan: Project Control Stages

437. Contracting method – what contracting method is to be used for the contracts?

438. Was your organizations estimating methodology being used and followed?

439. Was the scope definition used in task sequencing?

440. Are the payment terms being followed?

441. What is the work breakdown structure for the Project Control Stages project?

442. Does a documented Project Control Stages project organizational policy & plan (i.e. governance model) exist?

443. Are internal Project Control Stages project status meetings held at reasonable intervals?

444. Is it possible to track all classes of Project Control Stages project work (e.g. scheduled, un-scheduled, defect repair, etc.)?

445. Are key risk mitigation strategies added to the Project Control Stages project schedule?

446. Responsibilities – what is the split of responsibilities between the owner and contractors?

447. Is the structure for tracking the Project Control Stages project schedule well defined and assigned to a specific individual?

448. Are the people assigned to the Project Control Stages project sufficiently qualified?

449. Is current scope of the Project Control Stages project substantially different than that originally defined?

450. Has the schedule been baselined?

451. Contingency – how will cost contingency be administered?

452. Has a sponsor been identified?

453. Is the steering committee active in Project Control Stages project oversight?

454. Forecasts – how will the cost to complete the Project Control Stages project be forecast?

2.21 Activity Cost Estimates: Project Control Stages

455. Was it performed on time?

456. Does the estimator estimate by task or by person?

457. If you are asked to lower your estimate because the price is too high, what are your options?

458. Was the consultant knowledgeable about the program?

459. Were the costs or charges reasonable?

460. What is the estimators estimating history?

461. What is included in indirect cost being allocated?

462. Were sponsors and decision makers available when needed outside regularly scheduled meetings?

463. Performance bond should always provide what part of the contract value?

464. How do you manage cost?

465. Eac -estimate at completion, what is the total job expected to cost?

466. Is costing method consistent with study goals?

467. How many activities should you have?

468. How and when do you enter into Project Control Stages project Procurement Management?

469. What were things that you need to improve?

470. Estimated cost?

471. How quickly can the task be done with the skills available?

472. Will you use any tools, such as Project Control Stages project management software, to assist in capturing Earned Value metrics?

473. Will you need to provide essential services information about activities?

2.22 Cost Estimating Worksheet: Project Control Stages

474. Is it feasible to establish a control group arrangement?

475. What is the estimated labor cost today based upon this information?

476. Does the Project Control Stages project provide innovative ways for stakeholders to overcome obstacles or deliver better outcomes?

477. What is the purpose of estimating?

478. Who is best positioned to know and assist in identifying corresponding factors?

479. What costs are to be estimated?

480. Ask: are others positioned to know, are others credible, and will others cooperate?

481. What happens to any remaining funds not used?

482. What can be included?

483. How will the results be shared and to whom?

484. Is the Project Control Stages project responsive to community need?

485. Will the Project Control Stages project collaborate

with the local community and leverage resources?

486. Can a trend be established from historical performance data on the selected measure and are the criteria for using trend analysis or forecasting methods met?

487. What additional Project Control Stages project(s) could be initiated as a result of this Project Control Stages project?

488. Identify the timeframe necessary to monitor progress and collect data to determine how the selected measure has changed?

489. What will others want?

2.23 Cost Baseline: Project Control Stages

490. Are there contingencies or conditions related to the acceptance?

491. Has training and knowledge transfer of the operations organization been completed?

492. Does it impact schedule, cost, quality?

493. Has the documentation relating to operation and maintenance of the product(s) or service(s) been delivered to, and accepted by, operations management?

494. Is the requested change request a result of changes in other Project Control Stages project(s)?

495. On time?

496. Have the lessons learned been filed with the Project Control Stages project Management Office?

497. Does a process exist for establishing a cost baseline to measure Project Control Stages project performance?

498. When should cost estimates be developed?

499. Is the cr within Project Control Stages project scope?

500. How accurate do cost estimates need to be?

501. Has operations management formally accepted responsibility for operating and maintaining the product(s) or service(s) delivered by the Project Control Stages project?

502. What does a good WBS NOT look like?

503. Where do changes come from?

504. Vac -variance at completion, how much over/ under budget do you expect to be?

505. What is the most important thing to do next to make your Project Control Stages project successful?

506. What do you want to measure ?

507. Are procedures defined by which the cost baseline may be changed?

508. What weaknesses do you have?

2.24 Quality Management Plan: Project Control Stages

509. Account for the procedures used to verify the data quality of the data being reviewed?

510. What is the Difference Between a QMP and QAPP?

511. How does your organization ensure the quality, reliability, and user-friendliness of its hardware and software?

512. Was trending evident between audits?

513. How are new requirements or changes to requirements identified?

514. What are your organizations current levels and trends for the already stated measures related to customer satisfaction/ dissatisfaction and product/ service performance?

515. How many Project Control Stages project staff does this specific process affect?

516. Does the program conduct field testing?

517. How is staff trained?

518. Were the right locations/samples tested for the right parameters?

519. How are data handled when a test is not run per specification?

520. Are you following the quality standards?

521. Does the program use modeling in the permitting or decision-making processes?

522. Is it necessary?

523. How do you check in-coming sample material?

524. Do trained quality assurance auditors conduct the audits as defined in the Quality Management Plan and scheduled by the Project Control Stages project manager?

525. How does training support what is important to your organization and the individual?

526. How does the material compare to a regulatory threshold?

527. Is there a Quality Management Plan?

528. Are you meeting the quality standards?

2.25 Quality Metrics: Project Control Stages

529. Where did complaints, returns and warranty claims come from?

530. Can you correlate your quality metrics to profitability?

531. Was material distributed on time?

532. What are your organizations expectations for its quality Project Control Stages project?

533. How can the effectiveness of each of the activities be measured?

534. How effective are your security tests?

535. How should customers provide input?

536. What is the benchmark?

537. Was the overall quality better or worse than previous products?

538. Is quality culture a competitive advantage?

539. Who notifies stakeholders of normal and abnormal results?

540. What about still open problems?

541. Who is willing to lead?

542. Is there a set of procedures to capture, analyze and act on quality metrics?

543. Was review conducted per standard protocols?

544. Are documents on hand to provide explanations of privacy and confidentiality?

545. Are there already quality metrics available that detect nonlinear embeddings and trends similar to the users perception?

546. Which data do others need in one place to target areas of improvement?

547. Does risk analysis documentation meet standards?

2.26 Process Improvement Plan: Project Control Stages

548. Have storage and access mechanisms and procedures been determined?

549. Have the supporting tools been developed or acquired?

550. Everyone agrees on what process improvement is, right?

551. Modeling current processes is great, and will you ever see a return on that investment?

552. Are you making progress on the improvement framework?

553. What is quality and how will you ensure it?

554. Where do you want to be?

555. Have the frequency of collection and the points in the process where measurements will be made been determined?

556. Does your process ensure quality?

557. What is the test-cycle concept?

558. What actions are needed to address the problems and achieve the goals?

559. Who should prepare the process improvement action plan?

560. What personnel are the sponsors for that initiative?

561. Does explicit definition of the measures exist?

562. What personnel are the champions for the initiative?

563. Why do you want to achieve the goal?

564. To elicit goal statements, do you ask a question such as, What do you want to achieve?

565. If a process improvement framework is being used, which elements will help the problems and goals listed?

566. Purpose of goal: the motive is determined by asking, why do you want to achieve this goal?

567. The motive is determined by asking, Why do you want to achieve this goal?

2.27 Responsibility Assignment Matrix: Project Control Stages

568. Past experience – the person or the group worked at something similar in the past?

569. Are too many reports done in writing instead of verbally?

570. Most people let you know when others re too busy, and are others really too busy?

571. Budgeted cost for work scheduled?

572. Time-phased control account budgets?

573. Too many rs: with too many people labeled as doing the work, are there too many hands involved?

574. Are people encouraged to bring up issues?

575. Authorization to proceed with all authorized work?

576. Evaluate the impact of schedule changes, work around, etc?

577. What do people write/say on status/Project Control Stages project reports?

578. The anticipated business volume?

579. Does the scheduling system identify in a timely

manner the status of work?

580. Changes in the overhead pool and/or organization structures?

581. What do you need to implement earned value management?

582. Who is going to do that work?

583. All cwbs elements specified for external reporting?

584. Do you need to convince people that its well worth the time and effort?

585. Do others have the time to dedicate to your Project Control Stages project?

2.28 Roles and Responsibilities: Project Control Stages

586. How is your work-life balance?

587. Accountabilities: what are the roles and responsibilities of individual team members?

588. Are governance roles and responsibilities documented?

589. Is feedback clearly communicated and non-judgmental?

590. Are Project Control Stages project team roles and responsibilities identified and documented?

591. To decide whether to use a quality measurement, ask how will you know when it is achieved?

592. What should you do now to prepare for your career 5+ years from now?

593. What specific behaviors did you observe?

594. Do you take the time to clearly define roles and responsibilities on Project Control Stages project tasks?

595. Required skills, knowledge, experience?

596. Does your vision/mission support a culture of quality data?

597. Concern: where are you limited or have no authority, where you can not influence?

598. What areas would you highlight for changes or improvements?

599. Is the data complete?

600. Are your policies supportive of a culture of quality data?

601. Who is responsible for each task?

602. How well did the Project Control Stages project Team understand the expectations of specific roles and responsibilities?

603. What should you do now to prepare yourself for a promotion, increased responsibilities or a different job?

604. Have you ever been a part of this team?

605. Authority: what areas/Project Control Stages projects in your work do you have the authority to decide upon and act on the already stated decisions?

2.29 Human Resource Management Plan: Project Control Stages

606. Sensitivity analysis?

607. Do Project Control Stages project managers participating in the Project Control Stages project know the Project Control Stages projects true status first hand?

608. Quality assurance overheads?

609. Is a payment system in place with proper reviews and approvals?

610. What is this Project Control Stages project aiming to achieve?

611. Are vendor contract reports, reviews and visits conducted periodically?

612. Has the business need been clearly defined?

613. Has a Project Control Stages project Communications Plan been developed?

614. Is a pmo (Project Control Stages project management office) in place and provide oversight to the Project Control Stages project?

615. Have all necessary approvals been obtained?

616. Are milestone deliverables effectively tracked

and compared to Project Control Stages project plan?

617. Who needs training?

618. Do you have the reasons why the changes to your organizational systems and capabilities are required?

619. Are schedule deliverables actually delivered?

620. Are risk triggers captured?

621. Do all stakeholders know how to access this repository and where to find the Project Control Stages project documentation?

622. Is there an issues management plan in place?

623. Were the budget estimates reasonable?

2.30 Communications Management Plan: Project Control Stages

624. Who have you worked with in past, similar initiatives?

625. Where do team members get information?

626. What does the stakeholder need from the team?

627. What help do you and your team need from the stakeholder?

628. Are you constantly rushing from meeting to meeting?

629. What approaches to you feel are the best ones to use?

630. Do you feel a register helps?

631. What communications method?

632. What to know?

633. What steps can you take for a positive relationship?

634. Who is involved as you identify stakeholders?

635. Do you have members of your team responsible for certain stakeholders?

636. Are there too many who have an interest in some aspect of your work?

637. What is Project Control Stages project communications management?

638. What is the stakeholders level of authority?

639. Conflict resolution -which method when?

640. Are there potential barriers between the team and the stakeholder?

641. How did the term stakeholder originate?

642. Which stakeholders are thought leaders, influences, or early adopters?

643. How much time does it take to do it?

2.31 Risk Management Plan: Project Control Stages

644. How is risk monitoring performed?

645. Are flexibility and reuse paramount?

646. Is the customer willing to commit significant time to the requirements gathering process?

647. Is the customer technically sophisticated in the product area?

648. What is the likelihood?

649. Are formal technical reviews part of this process?

650. Why is product liability a serious issue?

651. Management -what contingency plans do you have if the risk becomes a reality?

652. Has something like this been done before?

653. Risk may be made during which step of risk management?

654. Is there anything you would now do differently on your Project Control Stages project based on this experience?

655. Which is an input to the risk management process?

656. Do you manage the process through use of metrics?

657. Are certain activities taking a long time to complete?

658. Technology risk: is the Project Control Stages project technically feasible?

659. Is Project Control Stages project scope stable?

660. What will drive change?

661. Financial risk -can your organization afford to undertake the Project Control Stages project?

662. Are you on schedule?

2.32 Risk Register: Project Control Stages

663. Which key risks have ineffective responses or outstanding improvement actions?

664. What action, if any, has been taken to respond to the risk?

665. Are there other alternative controls that could be implemented?

666. What is the reason for current performance gaps and do the risks and opportunities identified previously account for this?

667. What has changed since the last period?

668. How is a Community Risk Register created?

669. What are you going to do to limit the Project Control Stages projects risk exposure due to the identified risks?

670. Budget and schedule: what are the estimated costs and schedules for performing risk-related activities?

671. Market risk -will the new service or product be useful to your organization or marketable to others?

672. What should you do when?

673. What could prevent you delivering on the strategic program objectives and what is being done to mitigate corresponding issues?

674. Severity Prediction?

675. What are the assumptions and current status that support the assessment of the risk?

676. What should the audit role be in establishing a risk management process?

677. Assume the event happens, what is the Most Likely impact?

678. Can the likelihood and impact of failing to achieve corresponding recommendations and action plans be assessed?

679. Who needs to know about this?

680. Do you require further engagement?

681. Are there any gaps in the evidence?

2.33 Probability and Impact Assessment: Project Control Stages

682. How much is the probability of a risk occurring?

683. Mitigation -how can you avoid the risk?

684. What are the current requirements of the customer?

685. Workarounds are determined during which step of risk management?

686. Are the facilities, expertise, resources, and management know-how available to handle the situation?

687. What are the likely future requirements?

688. Your customers business requirements have suddenly shifted because of a new regulatory statute, what now?

689. My Project Control Stages project leader has suddenly left your organization, what do you do?

690. Have staff received necessary training?

691. Do the people have the right combinations of skills?

692. What are the risks involved in appointing external agencies to manage the Project Control Stages

project?

693. Are people attending meetings and doing work?

694. Are trained personnel, including supervisors and Project Control Stages project managers, available to handle such a large Project Control Stages project?

695. What will be the likely political situation during the life of the Project Control Stages project?

696. How would you assess the risk management process in the Project Control Stages project?

697. Will there be an increase in the political conservatism?

698. Is the delay in one subProject Control Stages project going to affect another?

699. Risk data quality assessment - what is the quality of the data used to determine or assess the risk?

700. Which of your Project Control Stages projects should be selected when compared with other Project Control Stages projects?

2.34 Probability and Impact Matrix: Project Control Stages

701. How do you manage Project Control Stages project Risk?

702. What changes in the regulation are forthcoming?

703. Do you know the order of planning yet?

704. Which risks need to move on to Perform Quantitative Risk Analysis?

705. Risk categorization -which of your categories has more risk than others?

706. During Project Control Stages project executing, a major problem occurs that was not included in the risk register. What should you do FIRST?

707. Has the need for the Project Control Stages project been properly established?

708. Amount of reused software?

709. How is the risk management process used in practice?

710. Mandated delivery date?

711. What is the probability of the risk occurring?

712. Can the Project Control Stages project proceed

without assuming the risk?

713. How much risk do others need to take?

714. What are the preparations required for facing difficulties?

715. Is the customer willing to participate in reviews?

716. Is the technology to be built new to your organization?

717. To what extent is the chosen technology maturing?

2.35 Risk Data Sheet: Project Control Stages

718. Will revised controls lead to tolerable risk levels?

719. What is the duration of infection (the length of time the host is infected with the organizm) in a normal healthy human host?

720. Potential for recurrence?

721. What can happen?

722. How can hazards be reduced?

723. Type of risk identified?

724. Is the data sufficiently specified in terms of the type of failure being analyzed, and its frequency or probability?

725. What is the chance that it will happen?

726. What was measured?

727. Do effective diagnostic tests exist?

728. What is the environment within which you operate (social trends, economic, community values, broad based participation, national directions etc.)?

729. During work activities could hazards exist?

730. How can it happen?

731. What were the Causes that contributed?

732. Has the most cost-effective solution been chosen?

733. What actions can be taken to eliminate or remove risk?

734. What do you know?

735. What can you do?

736. Has a sensitivity analysis been carried out?

737. What is the likelihood of it happening?

2.36 Procurement Management Plan: Project Control Stages

738. Is documentation created for communication with the suppliers and Vendors?

739. Are estimating assumptions and constraints captured?

740. Has a provision been made to reassess Project Control Stages project risks at various Project Control Stages project stages?

741. In which phase of the Acquisition Process Cycle does source qualifications reside?

742. Have all documents been archived in a Project Control Stages project repository for each release?

743. Is there a requirements change management processes in place?

744. Have all unresolved risks been documented?

745. Do all stakeholders know how to access the PM repository and where to find the Project Control Stages project documentation?

746. Are status reports received per the Project Control Stages project Plan?

747. How will the duration of the Project Control Stages project influence your decisions?

748. Is the steering committee active in Project Control Stages project oversight?

749. Are post milestone Project Control Stages project reviews (PMPR) conducted with your organization at least once a year?

750. Are vendor invoices audited for accuracy before payment?

751. Public engagement – did you get it right?

752. Have the procedures for identifying budget variances been followed?

753. Were Project Control Stages project team members involved in the development of activity & task decomposition?

2.37 Source Selection Criteria: Project Control Stages

754. What should a DRFP include?

755. When is it appropriate to conduct a preproposal conference?

756. What instructions should be provided regarding oral presentations?

757. When is it appropriate to issue a DRFP?

758. Are resultant proposal revisions allowed?

759. What are the special considerations for preaward debriefings?

760. Do you want to wait until all offerors have been evaluated?

761. How can solicitation Schedules be improved to yield more effective price competition?

762. With the rapid changes in information technology, will media be readable in five or ten years?

763. Has all proposal data been loaded?

764. How will you evaluate offerors proposals?

765. Who is on the Source Selection Advisory

Committee?

766. What should preproposal conferences accomplish?

767. Is a cost realism analysis used?

768. How should the solicitation aspects regarding past performance be structured?

769. Have all evaluators been trained?

770. If the costs are normalized, please account for how the normalization is conducted. Is a cost realism analysis used?

771. What should be the contracting officers strategy?

772. How much weight should be placed on past performance information?

2.38 Stakeholder Management Plan: Project Control Stages

773. Are internal Project Control Stages project status meetings held at reasonable intervals?

774. Detail warranty and/or maintenance periods?

775. Are the Project Control Stages project team members located locally to the users/stakeholders?

776. Is quality monitored from the perspective of the customers needs and expectations?

777. Do Project Control Stages project teams & team members report on status / activities / progress?

778. What inspection and testing is to be performed?

779. How many Project Control Stages project staff does this specific process affect?

780. Are Project Control Stages project team members involved in detailed estimating and scheduling?

781. If a problem has been detected, what tools can be used to determine a root cause?

782. Which risks pose the highest threat?

783. Are communication systems proposed compatible with staff skills and experience?

784. What is to be the method of release?

785. What training requirements are there based upon the required skills and resources?

786. Have Project Control Stages project team accountabilities & responsibilities been clearly defined?

2.39 Change Management Plan: Project Control Stages

787. Why would a Project Control Stages project run more smoothly when change management is emphasized from the beginning?

788. Readiness -what is a successful end state?

789. What can you do to minimise misinterpretation and negative perceptions?

790. Which relationships will change?

791. What does a resilient organization look like?

792. What new roles are needed?

793. Clearly articulate the overall business benefits of the Project Control Stages project -why are you doing this now?

794. How can you best frame the message so that it addresses the audiences interests?

795. What are you trying to achieve as a result of communication?

796. Will a different work structure focus people on what is important?

797. How do you gain sponsors buy-in to the communication plan?

798. Are there resource implications for your communications strategy?

799. What risks may occur upfront, during implementation and after implementation?

800. What work practices will be affected?

801. What risks may occur upfront?

802. Will you need new processes?

803. Has the training co-ordinator been provided with the training details and put in place the necessary arrangements?

804. How prevalent is Resistance to Change?

805. Is a training information sheet available?

3.0 Executing Process Group: Project Control Stages

806. After how many days will the lease cost be the same as the purchase cost for the equipment?

807. What type of information goes in the quality assurance plan?

808. Who will be the main sponsor?

809. It under budget or over budget?

810. When will the Project Control Stages project be done?

811. Does software appear easy to learn?

812. Contingency planning. if a risk event occurs, what will you do?

813. Will new hardware or software be required for servers or client machines?

814. Is the program supported by national and/or local organizations?

815. What are the main types of goods and services being outsourced?

816. How can software assist in Project Control Stages project communications?

817. When do you share the scorecard with managers?

818. What are the Project Control Stages project management deliverables of each process group?

819. If action is called for, what form should it take?

820. Who are the Project Control Stages project stakeholders?

821. Is the Project Control Stages project making progress in helping to achieve the set results?

822. How will you avoid scope creep?

823. Are the necessary foundations in place to ensure the sustainability of the results of the programme?

824. What are the critical steps involved in selecting measures and initiatives?

825. Do the products created live up to the necessary quality?

3.1 Team Member Status Report: Project Control Stages

826. What is to be done?

827. Is there evidence that staff is taking a more professional approach toward management of your organizations Project Control Stages projects?

828. Do you have an Enterprise Project Control Stages project Management Office (EPMO)?

829. Does the product, good, or service already exist within your organization?

830. Why is it to be done?

831. How much risk is involved?

832. Does every department have to have a Project Control Stages project Manager on staff?

833. When a teams productivity and success depend on collaboration and the efficient flow of information, what generally fails them?

834. The problem with Reward & Recognition Programs is that the truly deserving people all too often get left out. How can you make it practical?

835. How it is to be done?

836. Will the staff do training or is that done by a third

party?

837. Does your organization have the means (staff, money, contract, etc.) to produce or to acquire the product, good, or service?

838. What specific interest groups do you have in place?

839. How can you make it practical?

840. Are the attitudes of staff regarding Project Control Stages project work improving?

841. How will resource planning be done?

842. Are the products of your organizations Project Control Stages projects meeting customers objectives?

843. How does this product, good, or service meet the needs of the Project Control Stages project and your organization as a whole?

844. Are your organizations Project Control Stages projects more successful over time?

3.2 Change Request: Project Control Stages

845. How can changes be graded?

846. What is the relationship between requirements attributes and reliability?

847. Customer acceptance plan how will the customer verify the change has been implemented successfully?

848. How are the measures for carrying out the change established?

849. How does a team identify the discrete elements of a configuration?

850. Will all change requests be unconditionally tracked through this process?

851. Change request coordination ?

852. How does your organization control changes before and after software is released to a customer?

853. What needs to be communicated?

854. Have all related configuration items been properly updated?

855. Who can suggest changes?

856. What should be regulated in a change control operating instruction?

857. Have scm procedures for noting the change, recording it, and reporting it been followed?

858. Are there requirements attributes that are strongly related to the occurrence of defects and failures?

859. Are there requirements attributes that are strongly related to the complexity and size?

860. What type of changes does change control take into account?

861. Can static requirements change attributes like the size of the change be used to predict reliability in execution?

862. What must be taken into consideration when introducing change control programs?

863. How well do experienced software developers predict software change?

864. Will new change requests be acknowledged in a timely manner?

3.3 Change Log: Project Control Stages

865. Is the submitted change a new change or a modification of a previously approved change?

866. Should a more thorough impact analysis be conducted?

867. Is the requested change request a result of changes in other Project Control Stages project(s)?

868. Does the suggested change request seem to represent a necessary enhancement to the product?

869. Is the change request open, closed or pending?

870. Who initiated the change request?

871. Is this a mandatory replacement?

872. How does this relate to the standards developed for specific business processes?

873. How does this change affect scope?

874. When was the request approved?

875. Does the suggested change request represent a desired enhancement to the products functionality?

876. Will the Project Control Stages project fail if the change request is not executed?

877. Is the change request within Project Control Stages project scope?

878. How does this change affect the timeline of the schedule?

879. When was the request submitted?

880. Do the described changes impact on the integrity or security of the system?

881. Is the change backward compatible without limitations?

3.4 Decision Log: Project Control Stages

882. How do you know when you are achieving it?

883. What eDiscovery problem or issue did your organization set out to fix or make better?

884. Adversarial environment. is your opponent open to a non-traditional workflow, or will it likely challenge anything you do?

885. What are the cost implications?

886. Decision-making process; how will the team make decisions?

887. With whom was the decision shared or considered?

888. Meeting purpose; why does this team meet?

889. What is your overall strategy for quality control / quality assurance procedures?

890. It becomes critical to track and periodically revisit both operational effectiveness; Are you noticing all that you need to, and are you interpreting what you see effectively?

891. How do you define success?

892. What alternatives/risks were considered?

893. How does provision of information, both in terms of content and presentation, influence acceptance of alternative strategies?

894. Do strategies and tactics aimed at less than full control reduce the costs of management or simply shift the cost burden?

895. At what point in time does loss become unacceptable?

896. Which variables make a critical difference?

897. What makes you different or better than others companies selling the same thing?

898. How effective is maintaining the log at facilitating organizational learning?

899. Behaviors; what are guidelines that the team has identified that will assist them with getting the most out of team meetings?

900. What is the line where eDiscovery ends and document review begins?

901. How does an increasing emphasis on cost containment influence the strategies and tactics used?

3.5 Quality Audit: Project Control Stages

902. Does everyone know what they are supposed to be doing, how and why?

903. How does your organization know that its relationships with the community at large are appropriately effective and constructive?

904. How does your organization know that its Governance system is appropriately effective and constructive?

905. Statements of intent remain exactly that until they are put into effect. The next step is to deploy the already stated intentions. In other words, do the plans happen in reality?

906. Are measuring and test equipment that have been placed out of service suitably identified and excluded from use in any device reconditioning operation?

907. How does your organization know that its systems for communicating with and among staff are appropriately effective and constructive?

908. Health and safety arrangements; stress management workshops. How does your organization know that it provides a safe and healthy environment?

909. How does your organization know that its

planning processes are appropriately effective and constructive?

910. What are the main things that hinder your ability to do a good job?

911. How does your organization know that its security arrangements are appropriately effective and constructive?

912. How does your organization know that its financial management system is appropriately effective and constructive?

913. How does your organization know that its system for ensuring a positive organizational climate is appropriately effective and constructive?

914. How does your organization know that its relationships with relevant professional bodies are appropriately effective and constructive?

915. Have the risks associated with the intentions been identified, analyzed and appropriate responses developed?

916. Are the policies and processes, as set out in the Quality Audit Manual, properly applied?

917. If your organization thinks it is doing something well, can it prove this?

918. How does your organization know that the system for managing its facilities is appropriately effective and constructive?

919. How does your organization know that its systems for providing high quality consultancy services to external parties are appropriately effective and constructive?

920. Are training programs documented?

921. What has changed/improved as a result of the review processes?

3.6 Team Directory: Project Control Stages

922. Process decisions: do invoice amounts match accepted work in place?

923. Process decisions: is work progressing on schedule and per contract requirements?

924. Decisions: what could be done better to improve the quality of the constructed product?

925. Who will write the meeting minutes and distribute?

926. Who will report Project Control Stages project status to all stakeholders?

927. Contract requirements complied with?

928. Have you decided when to celebrate the Project Control Stages projects completion date?

929. Where should the information be distributed?

930. Does a Project Control Stages project team directory list all resources assigned to the Project Control Stages project?

931. How will you accomplish and manage the objectives?

932. Process decisions: are there any statutory or

regulatory issues relevant to the timely execution of work?

933. Who are your stakeholders (customers, sponsors, end users, team members)?

934. Who will talk to the customer?

935. Is construction on schedule?

936. Process decisions: how well was task order work performed?

937. Who is the Sponsor?

938. Who are the Team Members?

939. Process decisions: are contractors adequately prosecuting the work?

3.7 Team Operating Agreement: Project Control Stages

940. To whom do you deliver your services?

941. Do you record meetings for the already stated unable to attend?

942. How will your group handle planned absences?

943. Do you leverage technology engagement tools group chat, polls, screen sharing, etc.?

944. Do you listen for voice tone and word choice to understand the meaning behind words?

945. Are there the right people on your team?

946. Did you draft the meeting agenda?

947. Do you send out the agenda and meeting materials in advance?

948. Do you begin with a question to engage everyone?

949. Did you delegate tasks such as taking meeting minutes, presenting a topic and soliciting input?

950. Do you use a parking lot for any items that are important and outside of the agenda?

951. What are some potential sources of conflict

among team members?

952. What are the current caseload numbers in the unit?

953. Do you ensure that all participants know how to use the required technology?

954. What resources can be provided for the team in terms of equipment, space, time for training, protected time and space for meetings, and travel allowances?

955. Do team members need to frequently communicate as a full group to make timely decisions?

956. Have you set the goals and objectives of the team?

957. What is a Virtual Team?

958. Conflict resolution: how will disputes and other conflicts be mediated or resolved?

959. Are team roles clearly defined and accepted?

3.8 Team Performance Assessment: Project Control Stages

960. To what degree do all members feel responsible for all agreed-upon measures?

961. To what degree does the teams work approach provide opportunity for members to engage in open interaction?

962. To what degree are corresponding categories of skills either actually or potentially represented across the membership?

963. To what degree is there a sense that only the team can succeed?

964. How do you manage human resources?

965. Lack of method variance in self-reported affect and perceptions at work: Reality or artifact?

966. To what degree can team members vigorously define the teams purpose in considerations with others who are not part of the functioning team?

967. When does the medium matter?

968. How hard do you try to make a good selection?

969. To what degree do team members feel that the purpose of the team is important, if not exciting?

970. To what degree can team members meet frequently enough to accomplish the teams ends?

971. Does more radicalness mean more perceived benefits?

972. To what degree do members articulate the goals beyond the team membership?

973. Effects of crew composition on crew performance: Does the whole equal the sum of its parts?

974. To what degree are the skill areas critical to team performance present?

975. If you are worried about method variance before you collect data, what sort of design elements might you include to reduce or eliminate the threat of method variance?

976. To what degree do the goals specify concrete team work products?

977. To what degree does the teams purpose contain themes that are particularly meaningful and memorable?

978. To what degree will the approach capitalize on and enhance the skills of all team members in a manner that takes into consideration other demands on members of the team?

979. To what degree can the team measure progress against specific goals?

3.9 Team Member Performance Assessment: Project Control Stages

980. Are any governance changes sufficient to impact achievement?

981. How do you implement Cost Reduction?

982. What, if any, steps are available for employees who feel they have been unfairly or inaccurately rated?

983. What are they responsible for?

984. How will you identify your Team Leaders?

985. What are the evaluation strategies (e.g., reaction, learning, behavior, results) used. What evaluation results did you have?

986. What are top priorities?

987. What are acceptable governance changes?

988. In what areas would you like to concentrate your knowledge and resources?

989. What does collaboration look like?

990. Do the goals support your organizations goals?

991. Should a ratee get a copy of all the raters documents about the employees performance?

992. What stakeholders must be involved in the development and oversight of the performance plan?

993. Are any validation activities performed?

994. What innovations (if any) are developed to realize goals?

995. What are the key duties or tasks of the Ratee?

996. What entity leads the process, selects a potential restructuring option and develops the plan?

997. What qualities does a successful Team leader possess?

3.10 Issue Log: Project Control Stages

998. What is the status of the issue?

999. Who do you turn to if you have questions?

1000. Why multiple evaluators?

1001. Persistence; will users learn a work around or will they be bothered every time?

1002. Why not more evaluators?

1003. What is a change?

1004. What approaches do you use?

1005. Who reported the issue?

1006. What is the impact on the risks?

1007. In classifying stakeholders, which approach to do so are you using?

1008. What is the stakeholders political influence?

1009. How is this initiative related to other portfolios, programs, or Project Control Stages projects?

1010. Who were proponents/opponents?

4.0 Monitoring and Controlling Process Group: Project Control Stages

1011. Mitigate. what will you do to minimize the impact should a risk event occur?

1012. Is there adequate validation on required fields?

1013. How well did the chosen processes fit the needs of the Project Control Stages project?

1014. What is the timeline for the Project Control Stages project?

1015. Is progress on outcomes due to your program?

1016. Change, where should you look for problems?

1017. Are there areas that need improvement?

1018. How is agile Project Control Stages project management done?

1019. Is the program making progress in helping to achieve the set results?

1020. What input will you be required to provide the Project Control Stages project team?

1021. How was the program set-up initiated?

1022. How can you make your needs known?

1023. How many potential communications channels exist on the Project Control Stages project?

1024. Is it what was agreed upon?

1025. Do the partners have sufficient financial capacity to keep up the benefits produced by the programme?

1026. What resources are necessary?

1027. How well defined and documented were the Project Control Stages project management processes you chose to use?

4.1 Project Performance Report: Project Control Stages

1028. To what degree are the structures of the formal organization consistent with the behaviors in the informal organization?

1029. To what degree does the informal organization make use of individual resources and meet individual needs?

1030. To what degree does the teams approach to its work allow for modification and improvement over time?

1031. To what degree do the structures of the formal organization motivate taskrelevant behavior and facilitate task completion?

1032. To what degree does the formal organization make use of individual resources and meet individual needs?

1033. What degree are the relative importance and priority of the goals clear to all team members?

1034. To what degree does the information network provide individuals with the information they require?

1035. To what degree are the goals ambitious?

1036. To what degree are the goals realistic?

1037. To what degree will the team adopt a concrete, clearly understood, and agreed-upon approach that will result in achievement of the teams goals?

1038. To what degree can team members frequently and easily communicate with one another?

1039. How will procurement be coordinated with other Project Control Stages project aspects, such as scheduling and performance reporting?

1040. What is the PRS?

1041. To what degree do team members frequently explore the teams purpose and its implications?

1042. To what degree do team members articulate the teams work approach?

1043. To what degree does the teams work approach provide opportunity for members to engage in results-based evaluation?

1044. To what degree are the tasks requirements reflected in the flow and storage of information?

4.2 Variance Analysis: Project Control Stages

1045. How do you identify potential or actual overruns and underruns?

1046. How does the monthly budget compare to the actual experience?

1047. When, during the last four quarters, did a primary business event occur causing a fluctuation?

1048. Are the bases and rates for allocating costs from each indirect pool consistently applied?

1049. Why are standard cost systems used?

1050. Are your organizations and items of cost assigned to each pool identified?

1051. Are authorized changes being incorporated in a timely manner?

1052. What is the actual cost of work performed?

1053. Are there quarterly budgets with quarterly performance comparisons?

1054. Are there changes in the direct base to which overhead costs are allocated?

1055. Other relevant issues of Variance Analysis -selling price or gross margin?

1056. Contemplated overhead expenditure for each period based on the best information currently is available?

1057. Are all budgets assigned to control accounts?

1058. What is the performance to date and material commitment?

1059. Is all contract work included in the CWBS?

1060. What is the expected future profitability of each customer?

1061. Budgeted cost for work performed?

1062. Does the contractor use objective results, design reviews and tests to trace schedule performance?

1063. Are the actual costs used for variance analysis reconcilable with data from the accounting system?

4.3 Earned Value Status: Project Control Stages

1064. How does this compare with other Project Control Stages projects?

1065. What is the unit of forecast value?

1066. Validation is a process of ensuring that the developed system will actually achieve the stakeholders desired outcomes; Are you building the right product? What do you validate?

1067. If earned value management (EVM) is so good in determining the true status of a Project Control Stages project and Project Control Stages project its completion, why is it that hardly any one uses it in information systems related Project Control Stages projects?

1068. Where are your problem areas?

1069. Verification is a process of ensuring that the developed system satisfies the stakeholders agreements and specifications; Are you building the product right? What do you verify?

1070. Are you hitting your Project Control Stages projects targets?

1071. When is it going to finish?

1072. How much is it going to cost by the finish?

1073. Where is evidence-based earned value in your organization reported?

1074. Earned value can be used in almost any Project Control Stages project situation and in almost any Project Control Stages project environment. it may be used on large Project Control Stages projects, medium sized Project Control Stages projects, tiny Project Control Stages projects (in cut-down form), complex and simple Project Control Stages projects and in any market sector. some people, of course, know all about earned value, they have used it for years - but perhaps not as effectively as they could have?

4.4 Risk Audit: Project Control Stages

1075. Is your organization able to present documentary evidence in support of compliance?

1076. Does the customer have a solid idea of what is required?

1077. Do requirements put excessive performance constraints on the product?

1078. Who audits the auditor?

1079. Does the Project Control Stages project team have experience with the technology to be implemented?

1080. Do you ensure the recommended rules of play and protocols are followed for your activity?

1081. Are you willing to seek legal advice when required?

1082. Number of users of the product?

1083. Is the customer willing to establish rapid communication links with the developer?

1084. Are procedures developed to respond to foreseeable emergencies and communicated to all involved?

1085. Do you have an understanding of insurance claims processes?

1086. How do you compare to other jurisdictions when managing the risk of ....?

1087. Has risk management been considered when planning an event?

1088. Have customers been involved fully in the definition of requirements?

1089. Will safety checks of personal equipment supplied by competitors be conducted?

1090. How risk averse are you?

1091. What programmatic and Fiscal information is being collected and analyzed?

4.5 Contractor Status Report: Project Control Stages

1092. What are the minimum and optimal bandwidth requirements for the proposed soluiton?

1093. What was the overall budget or estimated cost?

1094. How is risk transferred?

1095. Who can list a Project Control Stages project as organization experience, your organization or a previous employee of your organization?

1096. What was the final actual cost?

1097. If applicable; describe your standard schedule for new software version releases. Are new software version releases included in the standard maintenance plan?

1098. What was the budget or estimated cost for your organizations services?

1099. Describe how often regular updates are made to the proposed solution. Are corresponding regular updates included in the standard maintenance plan?

1100. How does the proposed individual meet each requirement?

1101. How long have you been using the services?

1102. What process manages the contracts?

1103. What is the average response time for answering a support call?

1104. Are there contractual transfer concerns?

1105. What was the actual budget or estimated cost for your organizations services?

4.6 Formal Acceptance: Project Control Stages

1106. Do you buy-in installation services?

1107. What are the requirements against which to test, Who will execute?

1108. Did the Project Control Stages project manager and team act in a professional and ethical manner?

1109. Who would use it?

1110. Have all comments been addressed?

1111. Was the Project Control Stages project work done on time, within budget, and according to specification?

1112. Who supplies data?

1113. Is formal acceptance of the Project Control Stages project product documented and distributed?

1114. Was the Project Control Stages project managed well?

1115. What was done right?

1116. Was the client satisfied with the Project Control Stages project results?

1117. What features, practices, and processes proved

to be strengths or weaknesses?

1118. How does your team plan to obtain formal acceptance on your Project Control Stages project?

1119. Did the Project Control Stages project achieve its MOV?

1120. Do you perform formal acceptance or burn-in tests?

1121. Do you buy pre-configured systems or build your own configuration?

1122. Was the Project Control Stages project goal achieved?

1123. General estimate of the costs and times to complete the Project Control Stages project?

1124. What is the Acceptance Management Process?

1125. What function(s) does it fill or meet?

5.0 Closing Process Group: Project Control Stages

1126. What were things that you did well, and could improve, and how?

1127. Does the close educate others to improve performance?

1128. How well did you do?

1129. Were escalated issues resolved promptly?

1130. What level of risk does the proposed budget represent to the Project Control Stages project?

1131. What was learned?

1132. How will staff learn how to use the deliverables?

1133. How well defined and documented were the Project Control Stages project management processes you chose to use?

1134. How dependent is the Project Control Stages project on other Project Control Stages projects or work efforts?

1135. What is an Encumbrance?

1136. What communication items need improvement?

1137. Did the Project Control Stages project management methodology work?

1138. What were the actual outcomes?

1139. Were risks identified and mitigated?

1140. Was the user/client satisfied with the end product?

1141. What were the desired outcomes?

1142. What were things that you did very well and want to do the same again on the next Project Control Stages project?

5.1 Procurement Audit: Project Control Stages

1143. Have guidelines incorporating the principles and objectives of a robust procurement practice been established?

1144. Are there regular accounting reconciliations of contract payments, transactions and inventory?

1145. Is there no evidence of false certifications?

1146. Are risks in the external environment identified, for example: Budgetary constraints?

1147. Were results of the award procedures published?

1148. Did the contracting authority verify compliance with the basic requirements of the competition?

1149. Did the contracting authority offer unrestricted and full electronic access to the contract documents and any supplementary documents (specifying the internet address in the notice)?

1150. Was the admissibility of variants displayed in the contract notice?

1151. Does an appropriately qualified official check the quality of performance against the contract terms?

1152. Do procedures require cash advances to be returned by transferred or terminated employees before they can receive final paychecks?

1153. Did the conditions of contract comply with the detail provided in the procurement documents and with the outcome of the procurement procedure followed?

1154. In case of time and material and labour hour contracts, does surveillance give an adequate and reasonable assurance that the contractor is using efficient methods and effective cost controls?

1155. How do you address the risk of fraud and corruption?

1156. When tenders were actually rejected because they were abnormally low, were reasons for this decision given and were they sufficiently grounded?

1157. Do you learn from benchmarking your own practices with international standards?

1158. Is the performance of the procurement function/unit benchmarked with other procurement functions/units in the different stages of the procurement process?

1159. Are the right skills, experiences and competencies present in the acquisition workgroup and are the necessary outside specialists involved in part of the process?

1160. Is there an effective risk management system continuously monitoring procurement risk?

1161. Has a deputy treasurer been appointed to sign checks when the treasurer is unable to perform that duty?

1162. Are controls proportionated to risks?

5.2 Contract Close-Out: Project Control Stages

1163. What is capture management?

1164. Have all acceptance criteria been met prior to final payment to contractors?

1165. How is the contracting office notified of the automatic contract close-out?

1166. Has each contract been audited to verify acceptance and delivery?

1167. Are the signers the authorized officials?

1168. Have all contract records been included in the Project Control Stages project archives?

1169. Change in attitude or behavior?

1170. How/when used ?

1171. Was the contract sufficiently clear so as not to result in numerous disputes and misunderstandings?

1172. What happens to the recipient of services?

1173. Have all contracts been closed?

1174. Parties: who is involved?

1175. Parties: Authorized?

1176. How does it work?

1177. Have all contracts been completed?

1178. Change in knowledge?

1179. Change in circumstances?

1180. Was the contract type appropriate?

1181. Was the contract complete without requiring numerous changes and revisions?

5.3 Project or Phase Close-Out: Project Control Stages

1182. What process was planned for managing issues/ risks?

1183. In addition to assessing whether the Project Control Stages project was successful, it is equally critical to analyze why it was or was not fully successful. Are you including this?

1184. Planned remaining costs?

1185. Were cost budgets met?

1186. What are they?

1187. What is this stakeholder expecting?

1188. Is the lesson based on actual Project Control Stages project experience rather than on independent research?

1189. If you were the Project Control Stages project sponsor, how would you determine which Project Control Stages project team(s) and/or individuals deserve recognition?

1190. What stakeholder group needs, expectations, and interests are being met by the Project Control Stages project?

1191. Does the lesson educate others to improve

performance?

1192. What advantages do the an individual interview have over a group meeting, and vice-versa?

1193. What can you do better next time, and what specific actions can you take to improve?

1194. What was the preferred delivery mechanism?

1195. What information is each stakeholder group interested in?

1196. Does the lesson describe a function that would be done differently the next time?

1197. What information did each stakeholder need to contribute to the Project Control Stages projects success?

1198. Who controlled key decisions that were made?

5.4 Lessons Learned: Project Control Stages

1199. Who needs to learn lessons?

1200. Can the lesson learned be replicated?

1201. What were the problems encountered in the Project Control Stages project-functional area relationship, why, and how could they be fixed?

1202. How effective were the communications materials in providing and orienting team members about the details of the Project Control Stages project?

1203. How complete and timely were the materials you were provided to decide whether to proceed from one Project Control Stages project lifecycle phase to the next?

1204. How effectively and timely was your organizational change impact identified and planned for?

1205. How effectively were issues managed on the Project Control Stages project?

1206. What things surprised you on the Project Control Stages project that were not in the plan?

1207. How effective was the documentation that you received with the Project Control Stages project product/service?

1208. Did the Project Control Stages project change significantly?

1209. How useful was your testing?

1210. Is your organization willing to expose problems or mistakes for the betterment of the collective whole, and can you do this in a way that does not intimidate employees or workers?

1211. Was the Project Control Stages project manager sufficiently experienced, skilled, trained, supported?

1212. Were quality procedures built into the Project Control Stages project?

1213. How adequately involved did you feel in Project Control Stages project decisions?

1214. How to write up the lesson identified – how will you document the results of your analysis corresponding that you have an li ready to take the next step in the ll process?

1215. What was the methodology behind successful learning experiences, and how might they be applied to the broader challenge of your organizations knowledge management?

1216. Which estimation issues did you personally have and what was the impact?

1217. How many government and contractor personnel are authorized for the Project Control

Stages project?

Index

assets 116
assign 19
assigned   28-29, 131, 135, 138-140, 160, 212, 225-226
assigning   152
Assignment   4, 145, 173
assist   9, 61, 162-163, 199, 208
assistant   7
associated   128, 210
Assume   184
assuming   188
Assumption   3, 133
assurance   123-124, 140, 168, 177, 199, 207, 238
assure 45, 65
attainable   35
attempted   29
attempting   75
attend 214
attendance   28
attendant   60
attended   28
attending   186
attention   13, 86
attitude   240
attitudes   202
attribute   124, 133
attributes   3, 99, 144, 203-204
audiences   197
audited   192, 240
auditing   20, 79
auditor 229
auditors   168
audits 167-168, 229
auspices   8
author 1
authority   111, 123, 125-126, 176, 180, 237
authorized   137, 173, 225, 240, 245
automatic   240
available   18, 21, 28, 32, 43, 50, 54, 94, 140, 143, 153-154,
161-162, 170, 185-186, 198, 218, 226
Average   13, 23, 35, 48, 56, 69, 79, 109, 155, 232
averse 230
awareness   147
background 11, 114

Control1-6, 9-15, 17-23, 25-35, 37-44, 46, 48, 50-57, 59-63, 65-82, 84-93, 95-119, 121-127, 129, 131-169, 171, 173-183, 185-187, 189, 191-193, 195-197, 199-209, 212, 214, 216, 218, 220-229, 231, 233-237, 240, 242-245

controlled   53, 55, 243
controls   22, 50, 56, 63-64, 72, 75-78, 148, 183, 189, 238-239
convenient   42-43
convention   88
convey   1
convince   174
cooperate   163
Copyright   1
correct36, 70, 123
correction   137
corrective   74, 140
correlate   169
correspond   9, 11
corruption   238
costing42, 161
counting   102, 142
counts 102
course 29, 228
covered   112
covering   9, 76
coworker   96
crashing   149
craziest   98
create 11, 19, 47, 84, 97, 103, 131
created   53, 55, 92, 115, 124, 183, 191, 200
creating   7, 43, 119, 133
creativity   64
credible   163
crisis   18
criteria 2, 5, 9, 11, 21, 32-33, 35, 61, 77, 83, 87, 102, 110-111, 129, 131, 164, 193, 240
CRITERION   2, 17, 24, 36, 49, 58, 70, 81
critical 28, 32, 35, 53, 75, 78, 86, 95, 119, 146, 153, 200, 207-208, 217, 242
criticism   55
Crosby 153
crucial 52, 116
crystal 13
cultural59

making   22, 53, 59, 61, 98, 104, 106-107, 171, 200, 221
manage   46, 54, 96, 103, 112, 121, 129, 147, 161, 182, 185, 187, 212, 216
manageable   25
managed   7, 34, 233, 244
management   1, 3-5, 9, 11-12, 19, 26-28, 42, 47, 60, 63, 68, 70, 85-86, 103, 116, 121-125, 132-134, 138, 140, 145, 151, 155, 157-159, 162, 165-168, 174, 177-181, 184-187, 191, 195, 197, 200-201, 208-210, 221-222, 227, 230, 234-236, 238, 240, 245
manager   7, 12, 21, 30, 33, 96, 168, 201, 233, 245
managers   2, 110-111, 153-154, 177, 186, 200
manages   232
managing   2, 110-111, 115, 210, 230, 242
Mandated   187
mandatory   205
manner   111, 138, 153, 174, 204, 217, 225, 233
mantle 94
Manual   210
mapped   33
margin 225
market 42, 79, 116-117, 183, 228
marketable   183
marketer   7
Marketing   100, 104, 147
material   146, 168-169, 226, 238
materials   1, 214, 244
matrices   129
Matrix 3-5, 116, 129, 173, 187
matter 26, 43, 46, 216
maturing   188
maximizing   85
maximum   111
meaning   214
meaningful   38, 95, 217
measurable   26, 35, 100, 114
measure   2, 12, 19-20, 31, 36-41, 43, 45-47, 51, 56, 58, 60-61, 64, 66, 68, 74-76, 132, 164-166, 217
measured   21, 36, 38-44, 47, 62, 78-79, 169, 189
measures   37-40, 42, 44, 46-47, 51, 53, 56, 59, 71, 79, 119, 167, 172, 200, 203, 216
measuring   209
mechanical   1
mechanism   133, 243

mechanisms 118, 171
mediated 215
medium 216, 228
meeting 26, 42, 72, 112, 134, 168, 179, 202, 207, 212, 214, 243
meetings 25-28, 112, 131, 159, 161, 186, 195, 208, 214-215
megatrends 85
Member 5-6, 30, 102, 201, 218
members 25-27, 29, 33, 123, 153, 175, 179, 192, 195, 213, 215-217, 223-224, 244
membership 216-217
memorable 217
merely 116
message 197
method 33, 107, 145, 156, 159, 161, 179-180, 196, 216-217
methods 24, 32, 38, 44, 122, 134, 164, 238
metrics 4, 34, 36, 73, 162, 169-170, 182
milestone 3, 146, 148, 177, 192
milestones 27, 115
minimise 197
minimize 221
minimizing 85
minimum 27, 231
minutes 26, 62, 212, 214
missed 42, 84
missing 97, 144
mission 53, 55, 85, 92, 97, 99-100, 175
mistakes 245
Mitigate 184, 221
mitigated 236
Mitigation 159, 185
mobilized 118
modeling 55, 112, 168, 171
models 54, 91, 97
modified 59
module 157
moments 52
momentum 84, 87
monetary 19
monitor 65, 74-75, 77, 79, 154, 164
monitored 73, 143, 155, 195
monitoring 6, 72, 76, 150, 181, 221, 238
monthly 225

purchased   11
purpose   2, 11, 92, 131, 151-152, 163, 172, 207, 216-217, 224
pursued   87
pushing   91
qualified   25, 160, 237
qualifying   158
qualities   219
quality 1, 4-5, 11, 41, 45-46, 51, 53, 71, 73, 111-112, 118, 123-124, 131, 140, 153, 165, 167-171, 175-177, 186, 195, 199-200, 207, 209-212, 237, 245
quarterly   225
quarters   225
question   12-13, 17, 24, 36, 49, 58, 70, 81, 83, 117, 119, 172, 214
questions   7, 9, 12, 55, 155, 220
quickly 12, 49-50, 52, 162
radically   52
raising 118
raters   218
rather 101, 242
rational   138
reaching   94
reaction   218
reactivate   83
readable   193
Readiness   197
readings   79
realism 194
realistic   112, 121, 157, 223
reality 181, 209, 216
realize 219
realized   90
really   7, 97, 173
reason 93, 107, 183
reasonable   96, 121, 123, 141, 159, 161, 178, 195, 238
reasons   25, 178, 238
reassess   191
re-assign   144
rebuild 103
receive   9-10, 30, 47, 238
received   32, 103, 185, 191, 244
recently   11, 86

Sometimes   43
Source 5, 89, 191, 193
sources   51, 56, 59, 91, 214
special 77, 114, 193
specific   9, 19, 22, 26, 31, 35, 90, 132, 144, 146, 148, 150, 160, 167, 175-176, 195, 202, 205, 217, 243
specified   94, 137, 174, 189
specify 217
specifying   237
spoken 86
sponsor   19, 160, 199, 213, 242
sponsored   34
sponsors   18, 161, 172, 197, 213
stability 45, 132
stable   182
staffed 32
staffing 17, 73, 134
Stages 1-6, 9-15, 17-23, 25-35, 37-44, 46, 48, 50-57, 59-62, 65-69, 71-77, 79-82, 84-93, 95-119, 121-127, 129, 131-137, 140-169, 171, 173-183, 185-187, 189, 191-193, 195-197, 199-203, 205-207, 209, 212, 214, 216, 218, 220-225, 227-229, 231, 233-238, 240, 242-246
standard   7, 150, 170, 225, 231
standards   1, 11-12, 72, 100, 112, 123, 134, 137, 168, 170, 205, 238
started 9, 147
starting 12, 119
startup 95
stated   83, 99, 128, 167, 176, 209, 214
statement   3, 12, 67-68, 101, 131, 133
statements   13, 23, 27, 35, 48, 53, 56, 69, 79, 109, 131, 172, 209
static   204
status   5-6, 55, 141, 159, 173-174, 177, 184, 191, 195, 201, 212, 220, 227, 231
statute 185
statutory   212
steering   160, 192
storage   171, 224
strategic   94, 100, 184
strategies   98, 159, 208, 218
strategy   22, 65, 79, 92, 101, 105, 119, 123, 194, 198, 207
strengths   123, 147, 234
stress   209